180 CAKES

EVERY DAY & BAKES

180 CAKES EVERY DAY & BAKES

An irresistible collection of mouthwatering brownies, buns, bars, muffins, cookies, pies, tarts, teabreads, breads, cakes and gateaux shown in 180 photographs

Every tempting recipe is explained step by step, with cook's hints and tips, variations and complete nutritional information throughout

Edited by Martha Day

southwater

This edition is published by Southwater, an imprint of Anness Publishing Ltd, Hermes House, 88–89 Blackfriars Road, London SE1 8HA; tel. 020 7401 2077; fax 020 7633 9499

www.southwaterbooks.com; www.annesspublishing.com

If you like the images in this book and would like to investigate using them for publishing, promotions or advertising, please visit our website www.practicalpictures.com for more information.

UK agent: The Manning Partnership Ltd; tel. 01225 478444; fax 01225 478440; sales@manning-partnership.co.uk

UK distributor: Grantham Book Services Ltd; tel. 01476 541080; fax 01476 541061; orders@gbs.tbs-ltd.co.uk

North American agent/distributor: National Book Network; tel. 301 459 3366; fax 301 429 5746; www.nbnbooks.com

Australian agent/distributor: Pan Macmillan Australia; tel. 1300 135 113; fax 1300 135 103; customer.service@macmillan.com.au

New Zealand agent/distributor: David Bateman Ltd; tel. (09) 415 7664; fax (09) 415 8892

Publisher: Joanna Lorenz
Senior Managing Editor: Conor Kilgallon
Editors: Lucy Doncaster and Liz Woodland
Copy Editor: Jan Cutler
Design: SMI
Photographers: Karl Adamson, Edward Allwright, David Armstrong, Steve Baxter, James Duncan, John Freeman, Michelle Garrett, Amanda Heywood, Tim Hill, Don Last, Michael Michaels
Recipes: Alex Barker, Carole Clements, Roz Denny, Christine France, Shirley Gill, Patricia Lousada, Norma MacMillan, Sue Maggs, Janice Murfitt, Annie Nichols, Louise Pickford, Katherine Richmond, Hilaire Walden, Steven Wheeler, Elizabeth Wolf-Cohen
Food for Photography: Carla Capalbo, Carole Handslip, Wendy Lee, Sarah Maxwell, Angela Nilsen, Jane Stevenson, Liz Trigg, Elizabeth Wolf-Cohen
Stylists: Madeleine Brehaut, Maria Kelly, Blake Minton, Kirsty Rawlings, Fiona Tillett
Editorial Reader: Rosie Fairhead
Production Controller: Wendy Lawson

© Anness Publishing Ltd 2007

Previously published as part of a larger volume, *500 Cakes and Bakes*.

Main front cover image shows Angel Cake – for recipe, see page 58.

Ethical Trading Policy
Because of our ongoing ecological investment programme, you, as our customer, can have the pleasure and reassurance of knowing that a tree is being cultivated on your behalf to naturally replace the materials used to make the book you are holding. For further information about this scheme, go to www.annesspublishing.com/trees

Notes
Bracketed terms are intended for American readers.

For all recipes, quantities are given in both metric and imperial measures and, where appropriate, in standard cups and spoons. Follow one set of measures, but not a mixture, because they are not interchangeable.

Standard spoon and cup measures are level.
1 tsp = 5ml, 1 tbsp = 15ml, 1 cup = 250ml/8fl oz.

Australian standard tablespoons are 20ml. Australian readers should use 3 tsp in place of 1 tbsp for measuring small quantities.

American pints are 16fl oz/2 cups. American readers should use 20fl oz/2.5 cups in place of 1 pint when measuring liquids.

Electric oven temperatures in this book are for conventional ovens. When using a fan oven, the temperature will probably need to be reduced by about 10–20°C/20–40°F. Since ovens vary, you should check with your manufacturer's instruction book for guidance.

The nutritional analysis given for each recipe is calculated per serving or item, unless otherwise stated. If the recipe gives a range, such as Serves 4–6, then the nutritional analysis will be for the smaller portion size, i.e. 6 servings. Measurements do not include ingredients added to taste.

Medium (US large) eggs are used unless otherwise stated.

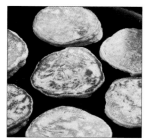

Contents

Introduction

Baking is one of the most satisfying of all the culinary arts. It fills the house with the most wonderful aroma, gives ample reward for minimal effort and always meets with approval, especially from younger members of the family.

This fabulous collection of over 180 recipes is all you need to earn your champion baker's badge. It ranges from simple teatime treats, such as drop scones and basic cookies, to cakes and gateaux. Each recipe is illustrated by a photograph of the finished result, and the step-by-step instructions are so simple and straightforward that even a beginner will find them easy to follow.

In fact, novice cooks often make the best bakers, preheating the oven in plenty of time, taking care to measure ingredients accurately and following recipe methods to the letter. All of these elements are important in baking, which demands more precision than many other types of cooking. It is well worth reading the chosen recipe carefully before you begin baking, as well as doing any preparation, such as browning almonds or softening butter, in advance, then setting out the measured ingredients in the style of the TV cook.

Advice on lining tins (pans) is given in individual recipes. Baking parchment is easy to use and gives excellent results, as it has a non-stick surface and it comes cleanly away from baked foods. To line a tin cut a piece of baking parchment a little longer than the circumference of the tin and 2.5cm/1in deeper. Fold over 2.5cm/1in along the long edge and snip up to the fold every 4cm/1½in or so. Use a pencil to draw round the base of the tin, then cut out a circle which is exactly the correct size to fit in the base of the tin. Grease the tin and line the sides with the baking parchment, so that the snipped edge lies on the base of the tin. Place the baking parchment circle in the base. For some recipes you will only need to line the base of the tin.

In this book there's a sweet or savoury treat for every taste and every moment of the day, from breakfast breads to a late-night slice of Pear and Hazelnut Flan, Chestnut and Orange Roulade or Chocolate Banana Cake. Tempted to embark on an immediate baking session? Go right ahead. Baking is a wonderfully therapeutic occupation – with sheer indulgence as the reward!

Caramel Meringues

Muscovado sugar gives these almost fat-free meringues a lovely caramel flavour. Take care not to overcook them, so that they stay chewy in the middle.

Makes about 20
115g/4oz/¹/₂ cup light muscovado (brown) sugar
2 egg whites
5ml/1 tsp finely chopped walnuts (optional)

1 Preheat the oven to 160°C/325°F/Gas 3. Line two baking sheets with baking parchment.

2 Press the muscovado sugar through a metal sieve into a large bowl positioned below.

3 Whisk the egg whites in a separate, grease-free bowl until they are very stiff and dry.

4 Add the sieved brown sugar to the stiff egg white, about 15ml/1 tbsp at a time, whisking well between each addition, until the meringue is thick and glossy.

5 Spoon small mounds of the meringue mixture on to the prepared baking sheets.

6 Sprinkle each mound of meringue mixture with chopped walnuts, if you like.

7 Bake the meringues for 30 minutes, then leave them to cool for 5 minutes on the baking sheets.

8 Transfer the meringues to a wire rack to cool completely.

> **Cook's Tip**
> For an easy, sophisticated filling, mix 115g/4oz/¹/₂ cup low-fat soft cheese with 15ml/1 tbsp icing (confectioner's) sugar. Chop 2 slices of fresh pineapple and add to the mixture. Sandwich the meringues together in pairs.

Snowballs

These light and airy morsels make a crisp and sweet accompaniment to low-fat frozen yogurt.

Makes about 20
2 egg whites
115g/4oz/¹/₂ cup caster (superfine) sugar
15ml/1 tbsp cornflour (cornstarch), sifted
5ml/1 tsp white wine vinegar
1.5ml/¹/₄ tsp vanilla extract

1 Preheat the oven to 150°C/300°F/Gas 2 and line two baking sheets with baking parchment.

2 Whisk the egg whites in a grease-free bowl, using a hand-held electric whisk, until very stiff.

3 Add the caster sugar, a little at a time, whisking after each addition until the meringue is very stiff and glossy. Whisk in the cornflour, vinegar and vanilla extract.

4 Using a teaspoon, mound the mixture into snowballs on the prepared baking sheets. Bake for 30 minutes.

5 Cool on the baking sheets, then remove the snowballs from the paper with a metal spatula.

> **Variation**
> Make Pineapple Snowballs by lightly folding about 50g/2oz/¹/₃ cup finely chopped semi-dried pineapple into the meringue.

> **Cook's Tip**
> These meringues contain the magic ingredients that give them a chewy centre rather than being crisp throughout. You can mix the cornflour, white wine vinegar and vanilla extract together in a small bowl and sprinkle it over the mixture before finally folding it in if you like.

Snowballs Energy 26kcal/113kJ; Protein 0.3g; Carbohydrate 6.7g, of which sugars 6g; Fat 0g, of which saturates 0g; Cholesterol 0mg; Calcium 3mg; Fibre 0g; Sodium 7mg.
Caramel Meringues Energy 26kcal/109kJ; Protein 0.4g; Carbohydrate 6g, of which sugars 6g; Fat 0.2g, of which saturates 0g; Cholesterol 0mg; Calcium 3mg; Fibre 0g; Sodium 6mg.

Apricot Yogurt Cookies

These soft-textured cookies are useful to give children in their lunchboxes, as they are low in fat and full of wholesome ingredients.

Makes 16

175g/6oz/1½ cups plain (all-purpose) flour
5ml/1 tsp baking powder
5ml/1 tsp ground cinnamon
75g/3oz/scant 1 cup rolled oats
75g/3oz/⅓ cup light muscovado (brown) sugar
115g/4oz/½ cup chopped ready-to-eat dried apricots
15ml/1 tbsp flaked (sliced) hazelnuts or almonds
about 150g/5oz/scant ⅔ cup natural (plain) yogurt
45ml/3 tbsp sunflower oil
demerara (raw) sugar, to sprinkle

1 Preheat the oven to 190°C/375°F/Gas 5. Lightly oil a large baking sheet.

2 Sift together the flour, baking powder and cinnamon. Stir in the oats, sugar, apricots and nuts.

3 Beat together the yogurt and oil, then stir evenly into the cookie mixture to make a firm dough. If necessary, add a little more yogurt.

4 Use your hands to roll the mixture into about 16 small balls, place on the baking sheet and flatten with a fork.

5 Sprinkle with demerara sugar. Bake for 15–20 minutes, or until firm and golden brown. Transfer to a wire rack to cool. Store in an airtight container.

> **Cook's Tip**
> *As these cookies have a moist texture they do not keep well, so it is best to eat them within 2 days. However, they freeze well. Pack them into plastic bags and freeze for up to 4 months. You can simply take one or two out to pop into a child's lunchbox as you need them.*

Oat and Apricot Clusters

These uncooked treats are full of flavour. You can change the ingredients according to what's in your cupboard – try peanuts, pecan nuts, raisins or dates.

Makes 12

50g/2oz/¼ cup butter or margarine
50g/2oz/4 tbsp clear honey
50g/2oz/½ cup medium oatmeal
50g/2oz/¼ cup chopped ready-to-eat dried apricots
15ml/1 tbsp banana chips
15ml/1 tbsp dried coconut shreds
50–75g/2–3oz/2–3 cups cornflakes or crispy cereal

1 Place the butter or margarine and honey in a small pan and warm over a low heat, stirring until well blended.

2 Add the oatmeal, apricots, banana chips, coconut and cornflakes or crispy cereal, and mix well.

3 Spoon the mixture into 12 paper cases, piling it up roughly. Transfer to a baking sheet and chill until set and firm.

Fruit and Nut Clusters

Children will love to help make these tasty morsels.

Makes 24

225g/8oz white chocolate
50g/2oz/⅓ cup sunflower seeds
50g/2oz/½ cup flaked (sliced) almonds
50g/2oz/½ cup sesame seeds
50g/2oz/⅓ cup seedless raisins
5ml/1 tsp ground cinnamon

1 Break the white chocolate into small pieces and melt in a heatproof bowl over a pan of simmering water.

2 Stir the melted chocolate until smooth and glossy. Mix in the sunflower seeds, flaked almonds, sesame seeds, raisins and cinnamon, and stir well. Using a teaspoon spoon the mixture into paper cases and leave in a cool place to set.

Yogurt Cookies Energy 104kcal/439kJ; Protein 2.3g; Carbohydrate 17.6g, of which sugars 5.8g; Fat 3.2g, of which saturates 0.4g; Cholesterol 0mg; Calcium 40mg; Fibre 0.7g; Sodium 10mg.
Oat and Apricot Energy 97kcal/407kJ; Protein 1.2g; Carbohydrate 11.7g, of which sugars 5.2g; Fat 5.4g, of which saturates 3.5g; Cholesterol 9mg; Calcium 7mg; Fibre 0.9g; Sodium 70mg.
Fruit and Nut Energy 93kcal/386kJ; Protein 2g; Carbohydrate 7.5g, of which sugars 7g; Fat 6.3g, of which saturates 2.1g; Cholesterol 0mg; Calcium 48mg; Fibre 0.5g; Sodium 12mg.

Apricot Specials

Walnuts complement the flavour of apricots perfectly in these fruity bars.

Makes 12

90g/3½oz/scant ½ cup soft light brown sugar
75g/3oz/⅔ cup plain (all-purpose) flour
75g/3oz/6 tbsp cold unsalted (sweet) butter, cut in pieces

For the topping

150g/5oz/generous ½ cup dried apricots
250ml/8fl oz/1 cup water
grated rind of 1 lemon
65g/2½oz/generous ¼ cup caster (superfine) sugar
10ml/2 tsp cornflour (cornstarch)
50g/2oz/½ cup chopped walnuts

1 Preheat the oven to 180°C/350°F/Gas 4. In a mixing bowl, combine the brown sugar and flour. With a pastry blender, cut in the butter until the mixture resembles coarse breadcrumbs, or rub in with your fingertips.

2 Transfer to a 20cm/8in square baking tin (pan) and press level. Bake for 15 minutes. Remove from the oven but leave the oven on.

3 To make the topping, place the apricots and water in a pan and simmer until the fruit is soft; about 10 minutes. Strain the liquid and reserve. Chop the apricots.

4 Return the apricots to the pan and add the lemon rind, caster sugar, cornflour and 60ml/4 tbsp of the soaking liquid. Cook for 1 minute.

5 Cool slightly before spreading the topping over the base. Sprinkle over the walnuts and bake for 20 minutes more. Cool in the tin before cutting into bars.

> ### Cook's Tip
> *Vary the dried fruit for these bars depending on what you have in your cupboard. Prunes and dried peaches work especially well.*

Brandy Snaps

You could serve these brandy snaps with rich vanilla ice cream rather than the cream filling.

Makes 18

50g/2oz/¼ cup butter, at room temperature
150g/5oz/¾ cup caster (superfine) sugar

20ml/1 rounded tbsp golden (light corn) syrup
40g/1½oz/⅓ cup plain (all-purpose) flour
2.5ml/½ tsp ground ginger

For the filling

250ml/8fl oz/1 cup whipping cream
30ml/2 tbsp brandy

1 Cream together the butter and sugar until light and fluffy, then beat in the golden syrup. Sift over the flour and ginger, and mix together. Transfer the mixture to a work surface and knead until smooth. Cover and chill for 30 minutes.

2 Preheat the oven to 190°C/375°F/Gas 5. Grease a baking sheet. Working in batches of four, shape the mixture into walnut-size balls. Place well apart on the baking sheet and flatten slightly. Bake until golden and bubbling, about 10 minutes.

3 Remove from the oven and leave to cool for a few moments. Working quickly, slide a metal spatula under each one, turn over, and wrap around the handle of a wooden spoon (have four spoons ready). If they firm up too quickly, reheat for a few seconds to soften. When firm, slide the brandy snaps off and place on a wire rack to cool.

4 When all the brandy snaps are cool, prepare the filling. Whip the cream and brandy until soft peaks form. Pipe into each end of the brandy snaps just before serving.

> ### Cook's Tip
> *Unfilled brandy snaps will keep well for up to 1 week if stored in an airtight container. However, you should eat filled brandy snaps as soon as they are made, as the cream softens them quite quickly.*

Apricot Specials Energy 169kcal/711kJ; Protein 1.8g; Carbohydrate 23.9g, of which sugars 18.3g; Fat 8.1g, of which saturates 3.5g; Cholesterol 13mg; Calcium 30mg; Fibre 1.1g; Sodium 41mg.
Brandy Snaps Energy 121kcal/505kJ; Protein 0.6g; Carbohydrate 11.7g, of which sugars 10g; Fat 7.9g, of which saturates 5g; Cholesterol 21mg; Calcium 16mg; Fibre 0.1g; Sodium 24mg.

Italian Almond Biscotti

Serve biscotti after a meal, for dunking in sweet white wine, such as an Italian Vin Santo or a French Muscat.

Makes 48
200g/7oz/1¼ cups whole unblanched almonds
215g/7½oz/scant 2 cups plain (all-purpose) flour
90g/3½oz/½ cup caster (superfine) sugar
a pinch of salt
a pinch of saffron powder
2.5ml/½ tsp bicarbonate of soda (baking soda)
2 eggs
1 egg white, lightly beaten

1 Preheat the oven to 190°C/375°F/Gas 5. Grease and flour two baking sheets.

2 Spread the almonds on an ungreased baking sheet and bake until lightly browned, about 15 minutes. When cool, grind 50g/2oz/½ cup of the almonds in a food processor, blender, or coffee grinder until pulverized.

3 Coarsely chop the remaining almonds into two or three pieces each. Set aside.

4 Combine the flour, sugar, salt, saffron powder, bicarbonate of soda and ground almonds in a bowl and mix to blend. Make a well in the centre and add the eggs. Stir to form a rough dough. Transfer to a floured surface and knead until well blended. Knead in the chopped almonds.

5 Divide the dough into three equal parts. Roll into logs about 2.5cm/1in in diameter. Place on one of the prepared baking sheets, brush with the egg white and bake for 20 minutes. Remove from the oven. Lower the oven temperature to 140°C/275°F/Gas 1.

6 With a very sharp knife, cut into each log at an angle making 1cm/½in slices. Return the slices on the baking sheets to the oven and bake for another 25 minutes. Transfer the biscotti to a wire rack to cool.

Orange Cookies

These classic citrus-flavoured cookies are ideal for a tasty treat at any time of the day.

Makes 30
115g/4oz/generous ½ cup butter, at room temperature
200g/7oz/1 cup caster (superfine) sugar
2 egg yolks
15ml/1 tbsp fresh orange juice
grated rind of 1 large orange
200g/7oz/1¾ cups plain (all-purpose) flour
15ml/1 tbsp cornflour (cornstarch)
2.5ml/½ tsp salt
5ml/1 tsp baking powder

1 Cream the butter and sugar until light and fluffy. Add the yolks, orange juice and rind, and continue beating to blend.

2 In another bowl, sift together the flour, cornflour, salt and baking powder. Add to the butter mixture and stir until it forms a dough. Wrap the dough in baking parchment and chill for 2 hours.

3 Preheat the oven to 190°C/375°F/Gas 5. Grease two baking sheets. Roll spoonfuls of the dough into balls and place 2.5–5cm/1–2in apart on the baking sheets.

4 Press down with a fork to flatten. Bake until golden brown, about 8–10 minutes. Using a metal spatula, transfer to a wire rack to cool.

Variation

These Orange Cookies are ideal for making into Orange Creams. Simply make a butter icing by creaming together 50g/2oz/ ¼ cup butter and 75g/3oz/¾ cup icing (confectioners') sugar until smooth. Add the grated rind of an orange and moisten to a spreadable consistency with a little freshly squeezed orange juice. Spread a little of the butter icing on to the flat side of a cookie and sandwich with another. Repeat with the remaining cookies. Chocolate butter icing would also go exceptionally well with the orange.

Biscotti Energy 51kcal/216kJ; Protein 1.6g; Carbohydrate 5.7g, of which sugars 2.2g; Fat 2.6g, of which saturates 0.3g; Cholesterol 8mg; Calcium 18mg; Fibre 0.4g; Sodium 5mg.
Cookies Energy 83kcal/350kJ; Protein 0.9g; Carbohydrate 12.6g, of which sugars 7.1g; Fat 3.6g, of which saturates 2.1g; Cholesterol 22mg; Calcium 15mg; Fibre 0.2g; Sodium 25mg.

Almond Tile Cookies

Light and delicate as a feather and truly delicious, these cookies make the perfect accompaniment to a creamy dessert.

Makes about 24

65g/2½oz/scant ½ cup whole blanched almonds, lightly toasted

65g/2½oz/5 tbsp caster (superfine) sugar
40g/1½oz/3 tbsp unsalted (sweet) butter, softened
2 egg whites
2.5ml/½ tsp almond extract
40g/1½oz/⅓ cup plain (all-purpose) flour, sifted
50g/2oz/½ cup flaked (sliced) almonds

1 Preheat the oven to 200°C/400°F/Gas 6. Thoroughly grease two baking sheets. Place the almonds and 30ml/2 tbsp of the sugar in a blender or food processor and process until finely ground, but not forming a paste.

2 Beat the butter until creamy, add the remaining sugar and beat until light and fluffy.

3 Gradually beat in the egg whites until the mixture is well blended, then beat in the almond extract.

4 Sift the flour over the butter mixture and fold in, then fold in the almond mixture.

5 Drop tablespoonfuls of the mixture on to the baking sheets 15cm/6in apart. With the back of a wet spoon, spread each mound into a paper-thin 7.5cm/3in circle. Sprinkle with the flaked almonds.

6 Bake the cookies, one sheet at a time, for 5–6 minutes, or until the edges are golden and the centres still pale.

7 Remove the baking sheet to a wire rack and, working quickly, use a metal spatula to loosen the edges of a cookie. Lift the cookie on the metal spatula and place over a rolling pin, then press down the sides of the cookie to curve it. Repeat with the remaining cookies, and leave to cool.

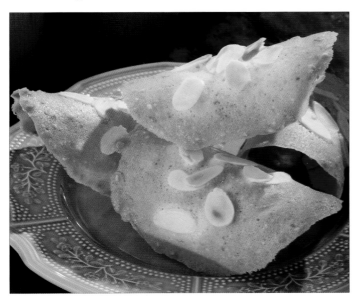

Ginger Florentines

These colourful, chewy cookies are delicious served with vanilla or other flavoured ice cream.

Makes 30

50g/2oz/¼ cup butter
115g/4oz/generous ½ cup caster (superfine) sugar
50g/2oz/¼ cup mixed glacé (candied) cherries, chopped
25g/1oz/generous 1 tbsp candied orange peel, chopped

50g/2oz/½ cup flaked (sliced) almonds
50g/2oz/½ cup chopped walnuts
25g/1oz/1 tbsp glacé (candied) ginger, chopped
30ml/2 tbsp plain (all-purpose) flour
2.5ml/½ tsp ground ginger

To finish

50g/2oz plain (semisweet) chocolate, melted
50g/2oz white chocolate, melted

1 Preheat the oven to 180°C/350°F/Gas 4. Beat the butter and sugar together until light and fluffy.

2 Add the glacé cherries, candied orange peel, flaked almonds, chopped walnuts and glacé ginger to the mixture, and blend thoroughly. Sift the plain flour and ground ginger into the mixture and stir well to combine.

3 Line some baking sheets with non-stick baking paper. Put four small spoonfuls of the mixture on to each sheet, spacing them well apart to allow for spreading. Flatten the cookies and bake for 5 minutes.

4 Remove the cookies from the oven and flatten with a wet fork, shaping them into neat rounds.

5 Return to the oven for about 3–4 minutes, until they are golden brown. Work in batches if necessary.

6 Let them cool on the baking sheets for 2 minutes to firm up, and then transfer them to a wire rack. When they are cold and firm, spread plain chocolate on the undersides of half the cookies and white chocolate on the undersides of the rest. Allow the chocolate to set before serving.

Almond Tile Energy 59kcal/246kJ; Protein 1.4g; Carbohydrate 4.5g, of which sugars 3.1g; Fat 4.1g, of which saturates 1.1g; Cholesterol 4mg; Calcium 16mg; Fibre 0.4g; Sodium 16mg.
Ginger Florentines Energy 71kcal/298kJ; Protein 0.9g; Carbohydrate 8.6g, of which sugars 7.8g; Fat 3.9g, of which saturates 1.3g; Cholesterol 2mg; Calcium 16mg; Fibre 0.3g; Sodium 11mg.

Sultana Cornmeal Cookies

These little yellow cookies come from the Veneto region of Italy, and contain Marsala wine, which gives them a rich flavour and enhances their regional appeal. Excellent served with a glass of wine.

Makes about 48
65g/2½oz/½ cup sultanas
  (golden raisins)
50g/2oz/½ cup finely ground
  yellow cornmeal
175g/6oz/1½ cups plain
  (all-purpose) flour
7.5ml/1½ tsp baking powder
a pinch of salt
225g/8oz/1 cup butter
200g/7oz/1 cup sugar
2 eggs
15ml/1 tbsp Marsala or
  5ml/1 tsp vanilla extract

1 Soak the sultanas in a small bowl of warm water for about 15 minutes. Drain.

2 Preheat the oven to 180°C/350°F/Gas 4, and grease a baking sheet. Sift the cornmeal and flour, the baking powder and the salt together into a bowl.

3 Cream the butter and sugar together until light and fluffy. Beat in the eggs, one at a time. Beat in the Marsala or vanilla extract.

4 Add the dry ingredients to the batter, beating until well blended. Stir in the sultanas.

5 Drop heaped teaspoonfuls of batter on to the prepared baking sheet in rows about 5cm/2in apart. Bake for 7–8 minutes, or until the cookies are golden brown at the edges. Remove to a wire rack to cool.

Cook's Tip
Marsala is a fortified wine with an alcohol level of around 20 per cent. There are sweet and dry types; use the sweet wine to give this recipe an authentic flavour.

Mexican Cinnamon Cookies

Pastelitos are traditional sweet shortbreads served at weddings in Mexico, dusted with icing sugar to match the bride's dress.

Makes 20
115g/4oz/½ cup butter
25g/1oz/2 tbsp caster
  (superfine) sugar
115g/4oz/1 cup plain
  (all-purpose) flour
50g/2oz/½ cup cornflour
  (cornstarch)
1.5ml/¼ tsp ground cinnamon
30ml/2 tbsp chopped
  mixed nuts
25g/1oz/¼ cup icing
  (confectioners') sugar, sifted

1 Preheat the oven to 160°C/325°F/Gas 3. Lightly grease a baking sheet. Place the butter and sugar in a bowl and beat until pale and creamy.

2 Sift the plain flour, cornflour and ground cinnamon into the butter and sugar mixture, and gradually work in with a wooden spoon until the mixture comes together. Knead the dough lightly until completely smooth.

3 Take tablespoonfuls of the mixture, roll into 20 small balls and arrange on the baking sheet. Press a few chopped nuts into the top of each one and then flatten slightly.

4 Bake the cookies for about 30–35 minutes, or until pale golden. Remove from the oven and, while they are still warm, toss them in the sifted icing sugar. Leave the cookies to cool on a wire rack before serving.

Cook's Tip
Choose two or three types of nut for this recipe. Cashew nuts, walnuts, raw skinned peanuts, almonds or hazelnuts all work well. Or choose from pecan nuts, pistachio nuts or macadamia nuts for a richer flavour. Make sure the nuts are chopped finely if small children are going to eat the cookies. You could even use some sesame seeds with the nuts if you like.

Sultana Cornmeal Energy 74kcal/311kJ; Protein 0.8g; Carbohydrate 8.9g, of which sugars 5.4g; Fat 4.2g, of which saturates 2.5g; Cholesterol 18mg; Calcium 10mg; Fibre 0.2g; Sodium 32mg.
Mexican Cinnamon Energy 91kcal/382kJ; Protein 0.8g; Carbohydrate 9.5g, of which sugars 2.8g; Fat 5.8g, of which saturates 3.1g; Cholesterol 12mg; Calcium 12mg; Fibre 0.2g; Sodium 37mg.

Lavender Cookies

Makes about 30
150g/5oz/²⁄₃ cup butter
115g/4oz/generous ½ cup caster
   (superfine) sugar
1 egg, beaten

15ml/1 tbsp dried lavender flowers
175g/6oz/1½ cups self-raising
   (self-rising) flour
leaves and flowers,
   to decorate

1 Preheat the oven to 180°C/350°F/Gas 4. Grease two baking sheets. Cream the butter and sugar together, then stir in the egg. Mix in the lavender flowers and the flour.

2 Drop spoonfuls of the mixture on to the baking sheets. Bake for 15–20 minutes, or until the cookies are golden. Serve with some fresh leaves and flowers to decorate.

Amaretti

Makes 36
200g/7oz/1¾ cups
   blanched almonds
plain (all-purpose) flour for dusting
225g/8oz/generous 1 cup caster
   (superfine) sugar

2 egg whites
2.5ml/½ tsp almond extract
icing (confectioners') sugar,
   for dusting

1 Preheat the oven to 160°C/325°F/Gas 3. Spread the almonds on a baking sheet and dry them out in the oven, without browning, for 15 minutes. Turn the oven off.

2 Leave the almonds to cool, then dust with flour. Grind with half the sugar. Whisk the egg whites until soft peaks form. Gradually whisk in half the remaining sugar until stiff peaks form. Fold in the remaining sugar, the almonds and the extract.

3 Pipe in walnut-sized rounds on to a greased baking sheet. Sprinkle with icing sugar and leave to stand for 2 hours. Preheat the oven to 180°C/350°F/Gas 4 and bake for 15 minutes. Cool on a wire rack.

Chocolate Amaretti

Although it is always said that chocolate does not go with wine, enjoy these delightful cookies Italian-style with a glass of chilled champagne.

Makes 24
150g/5oz/scant 1 cup blanched,
   toasted whole almonds

115g/4oz/generous ½ cup caster
   (superfine) sugar
15ml/1 tbsp unsweetened
   cocoa powder
30ml/2 tbsp icing
   (confectioners') sugar
2 egg whites
a pinch of cream of tartar
5ml/1 tsp almond extract
flaked almonds, to decorate

1 Preheat the oven to 160°C/325°F/Gas 3. Line a large baking sheet with non-stick baking paper or foil. In a food processor fitted with a metal blade, process the toasted almonds with half the sugar until they are finely ground but not oily. Transfer to a bowl and sift in the cocoa and icing sugar; stir to blend. Set aside.

2 Beat the egg whites and cream of tartar until stiff peaks form. Sprinkle in the remaining sugar 15ml/1 tbsp at a time, beating well after each addition, and continue beating until the whites are glossy and stiff. Beat in the almond extract.

3 Sprinkle over the almond mixture and gently fold into the egg whites until just blended. Spoon the mixture into a large piping (icing) bag fitted with a plain 1cm/½in nozzle. Pipe 4cm/1½in rounds, 2.5cm/1in apart, on the baking sheet. Press a flaked almond into the centre of each.

4 Bake the cookies for 12–15 minutes, or until they appear crisp. Remove the baking sheet to a wire rack to cool for 10 minutes. With a metal spatula, remove the cookies to the wire rack to cool completely.

> **Variation**
> As an alternative decoration, lightly press a few coffee sugar crystals on top of each cookie before baking.

Lavender Cookies Energy 74kcal/310kJ; Protein 0.8g; Carbohydrate 8.4g, of which sugars 4.1g; Fat 4.4g, of which saturates 2.7g; Cholesterol 17mg; Calcium 24mg; Fibre 0.2g; Sodium 54mg.
Amaretti Energy 37kcal/155kJ; Protein 1.1g; Carbohydrate 3.2g, of which sugars 3.1g; Fat 2.3g, of which saturates 0.2g; Cholesterol 0mg; Calcium 12mg; Fibre 0.3g; Sodium 4mg.
Chocolate Amaretti Energy 66kcal/278kJ; Protein 1.7g; Carbohydrate 7.2g, of which sugars 7g; Fat 3.6g, of which saturates 0.4g; Cholesterol 0mg; Calcium 19mg; Fibre 0.5g; Sodium 12mg.

Chocolate Delights

Simple and delicious, this method of making cookies ensures they are all of a uniform size.

Makes 50

25g/1oz plain (semisweet) chocolate
25g/1oz dark (bittersweet) cooking chocolate
225g/8oz/2 cups plain (all-purpose) flour
2.5ml/½ tsp salt
225g/8oz/1 cup unsalted (sweet) butter, at room temperature
225g/8oz/generous 1 cup caster (superfine) sugar
2 eggs
5ml/1 tsp vanilla extract
115g/4oz/1 cup finely chopped walnuts

1 Melt the chocolate in the top of a double boiler, or in a heatproof bowl set over a pan of gently simmering water. Set aside. In a bowl, sift together the flour and salt. Set aside.

2 Cream the butter until soft. Add the sugar and continue beating until the mixture is light and fluffy. Mix the eggs and vanilla extract, then gradually stir into the butter mixture. Stir in the chocolate, then the flour. Finally, stir in the nuts.

3 Divide the mixture into four equal parts, and roll each into a 5cm /2in diameter log. Wrap tightly in foil and chill or freeze until firm.

4 Preheat the oven to 190°C/375°F/Gas 5. Grease two baking sheets. With a sharp knife, cut the logs into 5mm/¼in slices. Place the circles on the baking sheets and bake until lightly coloured, about 10 minutes. Using a metal spatula, transfer to a wire rack to cool.

Variation

Try other nuts in this recipe, such as almonds, or use 50g/2oz/ scant ½ cup chopped ready-to-eat dried apricots, peaches or dates and halve the amount of nuts used. Almonds and apricots make a particularly pleasing combination, or try dates and pecan nuts.

Cinnamon Treats

Place these cookies in a heart-shaped basket, as here, and serve them up with love.

Makes 50

250g/9oz/2¼ cups plain (all-purpose) flour
2.5ml/½ tsp salt
10ml/2 tsp ground cinnamon
225g/8oz/1 cup unsalted (sweet) butter, at room temperature
225g/8oz/generous 1 cup caster (superfine) sugar
2 eggs
5ml/1 tsp vanilla extract

1 Sift the flour, salt and ground cinnamon together in a bowl. Set aside.

2 Cream the butter until soft. Add the sugar and continue beating until the mixture is light and fluffy. Beat the eggs and vanilla extract together, then gradually stir into the butter mixture. Stir in the dry ingredients.

3 Divide the mixture into four equal parts, then roll each into a 5cm/2in diameter log. Wrap the mixture tightly in foil and chill or freeze until it is firm.

4 Preheat the oven to 190°C/375°F/Gas 5. Grease two baking sheets. With a sharp knife, cut the logs into 5mm/¼in slices. Place the rounds on the baking sheets and bake until lightly coloured, about 10 minutes. Using a metal spatula, transfer to a wire rack to cool.

Variation

Transform these treats into sandwiched creams by making a chocolate orange butter icing. Cream together 50g/2oz/¼ cup butter and 75g/3oz/¾ cup icing (confectioner's) sugar until smooth. Add the grated rind of an orange. Blend 15ml/1 tbsp unsweetened cocoa powder with 15ml/1 tbsp water and add to the icing. Blend until smooth. Spread a little of the butter icing on to the flat side of a cookie and sandwich with another. Repeat with the remaining cookies.

Chocolate Delights Energy 90kcal/377kJ; Protein 1.1g; Carbohydrate 8.9g, of which sugars 5.5g; Fat 5.8g, of which saturates 2.7g; Cholesterol 17mg; Calcium 13mg; Fibre 0.2g; Sodium 31mg.
Cinnamon Treats Energy 71kcal/298kJ; Protein 0.8g; Carbohydrate 8.6g, of which sugars 4.8g; Fat 4g, of which saturates 2.4g; Cholesterol 17mg; Calcium 11mg; Fibre 0.2g; Sodium 31mg.

Coffee Sponge Drops

These light cookies are delicious on their own, but taste even better with a filling made by mixing low-fat soft cheese with chopped stem ginger.

Makes about 24

50g/2oz/ ¹/₂ cup plain
(all-purpose) flour
15ml/1 tbsp instant coffee powder

2 eggs
75g/3oz/6 tbsp caster
(superfine) sugar

For the filling (optional)

115g/4oz/ ¹/₂ cup low-fat
soft cheese
40g/1 ¹/₂oz/ ¹/₄ cup chopped
preserved stem ginger

1 Preheat the oven to 190°C/375°F/Gas 5. Line two baking sheets with baking parchment. Sift the flour and coffee powder together.

2 Combine the eggs and caster sugar in a heatproof bowl. Place over a pan of simmering water. Beat with a hand-held electric whisk until thick and mousse-like: when the whisk is lifted a trail should remain on the surface of the mixture for at least 30 seconds.

3 Carefully fold in the sifted flour mixture with a large metal spoon, being careful not to knock out any air.

4 Spoon the mixture into a piping (pastry) bag fitted with a 1cm/½in plain nozzle and pipe 4cm/1½in rounds on to the prepared baking sheets. Bake for 12 minutes. Cool on a wire rack.

5 Sandwich the sponge drops together in pairs with the filling or use a coffee icing, if you like.

> **Variation**
> To make Chocolate Sponge Drops, replace the coffee with 30ml/2 tbsp reduced-fat unsweetened cocoa powder.

Oaty Crisps

These high-fibre oat biscuits are quick and very easy to make. They are extremely crisp and crunchy – ideal to serve with morning coffee or as a tasty mid-afternoon snack.

Makes 18

175g/6oz/1¾ cups rolled oats
75g/3oz/ 6 tbsp soft light
brown sugar
1 egg
60ml/4 tbsp sunflower oil
30ml/2 tbsp malt extract

1 Preheat the oven to 190°C/375°F/Gas 5. Grease two baking sheets. Mix the oats and brown sugar in a bowl, breaking up any lumps in the sugar.

2 Add the egg, oil and malt extract, mix well, then leave to soak for 15 minutes.

3 Using a teaspoon, place small heaps of the mixture on the prepared baking sheets, leaving room for spreading. Press into 7.5cm/3in rounds with a dampened fork.

4 Bake the biscuits for 10–15 minutes, or until golden brown. Leave to cool for 1 minute, then remove with a metal spatula and cool on a wire rack.

> **Variation**
> Add 50g/2oz/ ¹/₂ cup chopped almonds or hazelnuts to the mixture. You could also add some jumbo oats to give a coarser texture.

> **Cook's Tip**
> As well as being low in fat these oaty cookies are healthy in other ways: oats are a healthy grain that contains soluble fibre, which is helpful in lowering blood cholesterol levels. As the grain does not contain gluten, oats are suitable for people who are gluten intolerant.

Sponge Drops Energy 33kcal/138kJ; Protein 1.5g; Carbohydrate 5.2g, of which sugars 3.6g; Fat 0.9g, of which saturates 0.4g; Cholesterol 17mg; Calcium 13mg; Fibre 0.1g; Sodium 27mg.
Oaty Crisps Energy 86kcal/364kJ; Protein 1.6g; Carbohydrate 12.8g, of which sugars 5.7g; Fat 3.6g, of which saturates 0.4g; Cholesterol 11mg; Calcium 9mg; Fibre 0.7g; Sodium 12mg.

Nutty Lace Wafers

Serve these delicate cookies with smooth and creamy desserts.

Makes 18

65g/2½oz/scant ½ cup blanched almonds
50g/2oz/¼ cup butter
40g/1½oz/⅓ cup plain (all-purpose) flour
90g/3½oz/½ cup caster (superfine) sugar
30ml/2 tbsp double (heavy) cream
2.5ml/½ tsp vanilla extract

1 Preheat the oven to 190°C/375°F/Gas 5. Lightly grease two baking sheets.

2 With a sharp knife, chop the almonds as finely as possible. Alternatively, use a food processor or blender to chop the nuts very finely.

3 Melt the butter in a pan over a low heat. Remove from the heat and stir in the flour, caster sugar, double cream and vanilla extract. Add the finely chopped almonds and mix well.

4 Drop teaspoonfuls 6cm/2½in apart on the prepared sheets. Bake until golden, about 5 minutes. Cool on the baking sheets briefly, just until the wafers are stiff enough to remove. With a metal spatula, transfer to a wire rack to cool.

> **Cook's Tip**
> *Many cookies, like these ones here, are soft when cooked but crisp up as they cool. Don't allow them to overcook because you expect them to be firm when they come out of the oven.*

> **Variation**
> *Add 40g/1½oz/¼ cup finely chopped candied orange peel to the mixture at step 3.*

Oat Lace Rounds

These nutty cookies are very quick and easy to make and they taste delicious.

Makes 36

165g/5½oz/⅔ cup butter or margarine
130g/4½oz/1¼ cups rolled oats
170g/5¾oz/generous ¾ cup soft dark brown sugar
155g/5¼oz/generous ¾ cup caster (superfine) sugar
40g/1½oz/⅓ cup plain (all-purpose) flour
1.5ml/¼ tsp salt
1 egg, lightly beaten
5ml/1 tsp vanilla extract
65g/2½oz/generous ⅓ cup pecan nuts or walnuts, finely chopped

1 Preheat the oven to 180°C/350°F/Gas 4. Lightly grease two baking sheets. Melt the butter or margarine in a medium pan over a low heat. Set aside.

2 In a mixing bowl, combine the oats, brown sugar, caster sugar, flour and salt. Make a well in the centre and add the butter or margarine, egg and vanilla. Mix until blended, then stir in the chopped nuts.

3 Drop rounded teaspoonfuls of the mixture about 5cm/2in apart on the prepared baking sheets.

4 Bake in the oven until lightly browned on the edges and bubbling all over, about 5–8 minutes. Cool on the baking sheets for 2 minutes, then transfer to a wire rack to cool completely.

> **Cook's Tip**
> *Rolled oats are also known as oatflakes and porridge oats. Fine oatmeal is also excellent for making cookies.*

> **Variation**
> *Substitute 5ml/1 tsp ground cinnamon for the vanilla extract for a tasty variation.*

Nut Lace Wafers Energy 78kcal/327kJ; Protein 1g; Carbohydrate 7.2g, of which sugars 5.5g; Fat 5.2g, of which saturates 2.2g; Cholesterol 8mg; Calcium 16mg; Fibre 0.3g; Sodium 18mg.
Oat Lace Rounds Energy 103kcal/432kJ; Protein 1g; Carbohydrate 13.2g, of which sugars 9.7g; Fat 5.5g, of which saturates 2.5g; Cholesterol 15mg; Calcium 11mg; Fibre 0.4g; Sodium 32mg.

Chocolate Walnut Bars

These delicious double-decker bars should be stored in the refrigerator in an airtight container.

Makes 24
50g/2oz/⅓ cup walnuts
55g/2¼oz/generous ¼ cup caster (superfine) sugar
100g/3¾oz/scant 1 cup plain (all-purpose) flour, sifted
90g/3½oz/7 tbsp cold unsalted (sweet) butter, cut into pieces

For the topping
25g/1oz/2 tbsp unsalted (sweet) butter
90ml/6 tbsp water
25g/1oz/¼ cup unsweetened cocoa powder
90g/3½oz/½ cup caster (superfine) sugar
5ml/1 tsp vanilla extract
1.5ml/¼ tsp salt
2 eggs
icing (confectioners') sugar, for dusting

1 Preheat the oven to 180°C/350°F/Gas 4. Grease the base and sides of a 20cm/8in square baking tin (pan).

2 Grind the walnuts with a few tablespoons of the caster sugar in a food processor or blender. In a bowl, combine the ground walnuts, remaining sugar and the flour.

3 Rub in the butter using your fingertips or a pastry cutter until the mixture resembles coarse breadcrumbs. Alternatively, use a food processor.

4 Pat the walnut mixture evenly into the base of the baking tin. Bake for 25 minutes.

5 To make the topping, melt the butter with the water. Whisk in the cocoa powder and sugar. Remove from the heat, stir in the vanilla extract and salt, then cool for 5 minutes.

6 Whisk in the eggs until blended. Pour the topping over the baked crust.

7 Return to the oven and bake until set, about 20 minutes. Set the tin on a wire rack to cool, then cut into bars and dust with icing sugar before serving.

Hazelnut Squares

These crunchy, nutty squares are made in a single bowl. What could be simpler?

Makes 9
50g/2oz plain (semisweet) chocolate
65g/2½oz/5 tbsp butter or margarine
225g/8oz/generous 1 cup caster (superfine) sugar
50g/2oz/½ cup plain (all-purpose) flour
2.5ml/½ tsp baking powder
2 eggs, beaten
2.5ml/½ tsp vanilla extract
115g/4oz/1 cup skinned hazelnuts, roughly chopped

1 Preheat the oven to 180°C/350°F/Gas 4. Grease a 20cm/8in square baking tin (pan).

2 In a heatproof bowl set over a pan of barely simmering water, melt the chocolate and butter or margarine. Remove the bowl from the heat.

3 Add the sugar, flour, baking powder, eggs, vanilla extract and half of the hazelnuts to the melted mixture and stir well with a wooden spoon.

4 Pour the mixture into the prepared tin. Bake in the oven for 10 minutes, then sprinkle the reserved hazelnuts over the top. Return to the oven and continue baking until firm to the touch, about 25 minutes.

5 Cool in the tin set on a wire rack for 10 minutes, then unmould on to the rack and cool completely. Cut into squares before serving.

> **Cook's Tip**
> To remove the skins from the hazelnuts put them on a foil-covered grill (broiling) pan and lightly toast them under the grill on a high heat until the skins loosen. Make sure that the hazelnuts do not brown too much or they will overcook when the Hazelnut Squares are baked in the oven.

Bars Energy 97kcal/407kJ; Protein 1.5g; Carbohydrate 9.8g, of which sugars 6.5g; Fat 6.1g, of which saturates 2.9g; Cholesterol 26mg; Calcium 16mg; Fibre 0.3g; Sodium 45mg.
Squares Energy 299kcal/1252kJ; Protein 4.2g; Carbohydrate 34.8g, of which sugars 30.2g; Fat 16.9g, of which saturates 5.7g; Cholesterol 58mg; Calcium 48mg; Fibre 1.1g; Sodium 62mg.

Lemon Sponge Fingers

These dainty sponge fingers are perfect for serving with fruit salads or light, low-fat creamy desserts.

Makes about 20
2 eggs
75g/3oz/6 tbsp caster (superfine) sugar
grated rind of 1 lemon
50g/2oz/½ cup plain (all-purpose) flour, sifted
caster (superfine) sugar, for sprinkling

1 Preheat the oven to 190°C/375°F/Gas 5. Line two baking sheets with baking parchment.

2 Whisk the eggs, sugar and lemon rind together with a hand-held electric whisk until thick and mousse-like: when the whisk is lifted, a trail should remain on the surface of the mixture for at least 30 seconds.

3 Carefully fold in the flour with a large metal spoon using a figure-of-eight action.

4 Place the mixture in a piping (pastry) bag fitted with a 1cm/½in plain nozzle. Pipe into finger lengths on the prepared baking sheets, leaving room for spreading.

5 Sprinkle the fingers with caster sugar. Bake for 6–8 minutes until golden brown, then remove to a wire rack to cool.

Variation
To make Hazelnut Fingers, omit the lemon rind and fold in 25g/1oz/¼ cup toasted ground hazelnuts and 5ml/1 tsp mixed (apple pie) spice with the flour.

Cook's Tip
These delicate sponge fingers also make a good base for a rich sherry trifle if you are not watching your fat intake.

Apricot and Almond Fingers

These delicious high-fibre almond fingers will stay moist for several days, thanks to the addition of the apricots.

Makes 18
225g/8oz/2 cups self-raising (self-rising) flour
115g/4oz/½ cup soft light brown sugar
50g/2oz/½ cup semolina
175g/6oz/1 cup ready-to-eat dried apricots, chopped
30ml/2 tbsp clear honey
30ml/2 tbsp malt extract
2 eggs, beaten
60ml/4 tbsp skimmed milk
60ml/4 tbsp sunflower oil
a few drops of almond extract
30ml/2 tbsp flaked (sliced) almonds

1 Preheat the oven to 160°C/325°F/Gas 3. Grease and line a 28 x 18cm/11 x 7in baking tin (pan).

2 Sift the flour into a large bowl and stir in the sugar, semolina and apricots. Make a well in the centre and add the honey, malt extract, eggs, milk, oil and almond extract. Mix well until combined.

3 Turn the mixture into the prepared tin, spread to the edges and sprinkle with the flaked almonds.

4 Bake for 30–35 minutes, or until the centre springs back when lightly pressed. Invert the cake on a wire rack to cool. Remove the lining paper if necessary and cut into 18 slices with a sharp knife.

Cook's Tips
• If you cannot find ready-to-eat dried apricots, soak chopped dried apricots in boiling water for 1 hour, then drain them and add to the mixture. This works well with other dried fruit too. Try ready-to-eat dried pears or peaches for a change.
• As well as going extremely well with coffee these fingers will also make a tasty low-fat dessert served with a low-fat ice cream or frozen yogurt.

Lemon Sponge Fingers Energy 31kcal/131kJ; Protein 0.9g; Carbohydrate 5.9g, of which sugars 4g; Fat 0.6g, of which saturates 0.2g; Cholesterol 19mg; Calcium 8mg; Fibre 0.1g; Sodium 7mg.
Almond Fingers Energy 140kcal/589kJ; Protein 3.1g; Carbohydrate 23.6g, of which sugars 11.9g; Fat 4.3g, of which saturates 0.6g; Cholesterol 21mg; Calcium 40mg; Fibre 1.2g; Sodium 13mg.

Chewy Fruit Muesli Slice

The apricots give these slices a wonderful chewy texture and the apple keeps them moist.

Makes 8
75g/3oz/scant ½ cup ready-to-eat dried apricots, chopped
1 eating apple, cored and grated
150g/5oz/1¼ cups Swiss-style muesli
150ml/¼ pint/⅔ cup apple juice
15g/½oz/1 tbsp sunflower margarine

1 Preheat the oven to 190°C/375°F/Gas 5. Grease a 20cm/8in round cake tin. Combine all the ingredients in a large bowl.

2 Press the mixture into the tin and bake for 35–40 minutes, or until lightly browned and firm. Mark the muesli slice into wedges and leave to cool in the tin.

Mincemeat Wedges

Makes 12
225g/8oz/2 cups self-raising (self-rising) wholemeal (whole-wheat) flour
75g/3oz/6 tbsp unsalted (sweet) butter, diced
75g/3oz/⅓ cup demerara (raw) sugar
1 egg, beaten
115g/4oz/⅓ cup good quality mincemeat
about 60ml/4 tbsp milk
crushed brown or white café (sugar) cubes or a mixture, for sprinkling

1 Preheat the oven to 200°C/400°F/Gas 6. Line the base of a 20cm/8in round sandwich tin (layer pan) and lightly grease the sides.

2 Rub the butter into the flour, using your fingertips or a pastry cutter. Stir in the sugar, egg and mincemeat. Add enough milk to make a soft dough. Spread evenly in the prepared tin and sprinkled over the crushed sugar. Bake for 20 minutes, or until firm. Cool in the tin then cut into wedges.

Chocolate Raspberry Macaroon Bars

Any seedless preserve, such as strawberry or apricot, can be substituted for the raspberry in this recipe.

Makes 16–18
115g/4oz/½ cup unsalted (sweet) butter, softened
50g/2oz/½ cup icing (confectioners') sugar
25g/1oz/¼ cup unsweetened cocoa powder
a pinch of salt
5ml/1 tsp almond extract
115g/4oz/1 cup plain (all-purpose) flour

For the topping
150g/5oz/½ cup seedless raspberry preserve
15ml/1 tbsp raspberry flavour liqueur
175g/6oz/1 cup milk chocolate chips
175g/6oz/1½ cups finely ground almonds
4 egg whites
a pinch of salt
200g/7oz/1 cup caster (superfine) sugar
2.5ml/½ tsp almond extract
50g/2oz/½ cup flaked (sliced) almonds

1 Preheat the oven to 160°C/325°F/Gas 3. Line a 23 × 33cm/9 × 13in baking tin (pan) with foil and then grease the foil. Beat together the butter, sugar, cocoa and salt until blended. Beat in the almond extract and flour to make a crumbly dough.

2 Turn the dough into the tin and smooth the surface. Prick all over with a fork. Bake for 20 minutes, or until just set. Remove the tin from the oven and increase the temperature to 190°C/375°F/Gas 5.

3 To make the topping, combine the raspberry preserve and liqueur. Spread over the cooked crust, then sprinkle with the chocolate chips.

4 In a food processor fitted with a metal blade, process the almonds, egg whites, salt, caster sugar and almond extract. Pour this mixture over the jam layer, spreading evenly. Sprinkle with almonds.

5 Bake for 20–25 minutes, or until the top is golden and puffed. Cool in the tin for 20 minutes. Carefully remove from the tin and cool completely. Peel off the foil and cut into bars.

Muesli Slice Energy 107kcal/453kJ; Protein 2.3g; Carbohydrate 19.6g, of which sugars 11g; Fat 2.9g, of which saturates 1.1g; Cholesterol 4mg; Calcium 30mg; Fibre 1.9g; Sodium 85mg.
Mincemeat Wedges Energy 168kcal/707kJ; Protein 2.5g; Carbohydrate 26.9g, of which sugars 13g; Fat 6.3g, of which saturates 3.5g; Cholesterol 30mg; Calcium 82mg; Fibre 0.7g; Sodium 116mg.
Macaroon Bars Energy 266kcal/1115kJ; Protein 4.5g; Carbohydrate 32.1g, of which sugars 26.6g; Fat 14.1g, of which saturates 5.7g; Cholesterol 16mg; Calcium 66mg; Fibre 1.2g; Sodium 79mg.

Sticky Date and Apple Bars

If possible allow these healthy and tempting bars to mature for 1–2 days before cutting – the mixture will get stickier and even more delicious!

Makes 16
115g/4oz/½ cup butter
  or margarine
50g/2oz/⅓ cup soft dark
  brown sugar
50g/2oz/4 tbsp golden (light
  corn) syrup
115g/4oz/⅔ cup chopped dates
115g/4oz/generous 1 cup
  rolled oats
115g/4oz/1 cup wholemeal self-
  raising (self-rising) flour
225g/8oz/2 eating apples, peeled,
  cored and grated
5–10ml/1–2 tsp lemon juice
20–25 walnut halves

1 Preheat the oven to 190°C/375°F/Gas 5. Line an 18–20cm/ 7–8in square or rectangular loose-based cake tin (pan) with baking parchment. In a large pan, heat the butter or margarine, sugar, syrup and dates, stirring until the dates soften completely.

2 Gradually work in the oats, flour, apples and lemon juice until well mixed. Spoon into the tin and spread out evenly. Top with the walnut halves.

3 Bake for 30 minutes, then reduce the temperature to 160°C/325°F/Gas 3 and bake for 10–20 minutes more, or until firm to the touch and golden.

4 Cut into squares or bars while still warm, or allow to cool uncut then wrap in foil when nearly cold and keep for 1–2 days before eating.

> ### Variation
> *Oranges and dates are also a favourite and tasty combination. To make Sticky Date and Orange Bars, finely chop half an orange, including the peel. Add to the pan at step 1 with the dates and syrup, and cook with the dates until soft. Continue with the recipe but omit the apple and lemon juice.*

Blueberry Streusel Slice

If you are short of time, use ready-made pastry for this delightful summer streusel.

Makes 30
225g/8oz shortcrust pastry
50g/2oz/½ cup plain
  (all-purpose) flour
1.5ml/¼ tsp baking powder
40g/1½oz/3 tbsp butter
  or margarine
25g/1oz/2 tbsp fresh white
  breadcrumbs
50g/2oz/¼ cup soft light
  brown sugar
1.5ml/¼ tsp salt
50g/2oz/½ cup flaked (sliced) or
  chopped almonds
30ml/4 tbsp blackberry or
  bramble jelly
115g/4oz/1 cup blueberries,
  fresh or frozen

1 Preheat the oven to 180°C/350°F/Gas 4. Line an 18 x 28cm/ 7 x 11in Swiss roll tin (jelly roll pan) with baking parchment. Roll out the pastry on a lightly floured surface and place in the tin. Prick the base evenly with a fork.

2 Rub together the plain flour, baking powder, butter or margarine, breadcrumbs, sugar and salt until very crumbly, then mix in the almonds.

3 Spread the pastry with the jelly, sprinkle with the blueberries, then cover evenly with the streusel topping, pressing down lightly. Bake for 30–40 minutes, reducing the temperature after 20 minutes to 160°C/325°F/Gas 3.

4 Remove from the oven when golden on the top and the pastry is cooked through. Cut into slices while still hot, then allow to cool.

> ### Variations
> *Another summer fruit that would work well is the strawberry. If using strawberries, substitute a good strawberry conserve for the blackberry or bramble jelly. You could still enjoy this streusel slice in autumn with the season's blackberries, which will go perfectly with the bramble jelly.*

Streusel Slice Energy 73kcal/304kJ; Protein 1.1g; Carbohydrate 8.2g, of which sugars 2.8g; Fat 4.2g, of which saturates 1.4g; Cholesterol 4mg; Calcium 17mg; Fibre 0.5g; Sodium 45mg.
Bars Energy 195kcal/815kJ; Protein 2.8g; Carbohydrate 22.8g, of which sugars 12.2g; Fat 10.9g, of which saturates 0.4g; Cholesterol 0mg; Calcium 41mg; Fibre 1.4g; Sodium 96mg.

Spiced Fig Bars

Make sure you have napkins handy when you serve these deliciously sticky bars.

Makes 48
350g/12oz/2 cups dried figs
3 eggs
175g/6oz/scant 1 cup caster
 (superfine) sugar
75g/3oz/⅔ cup plain
 (all-purpose) flour
5ml/1 tsp baking powder
2.5ml/½ tsp ground cinnamon
1.5ml/¼ tsp ground cloves
1.5ml/¼ tsp freshly
 grated nutmeg
1.5ml/¼ tsp salt
75g/3oz/¾ cup finely
 chopped walnuts
30ml/2 tbsp brandy or cognac
icing (confectioners') sugar,
 for dusting

1 Preheat the oven to 160°C/325°F/Gas 3. Then line a 30 x 20 x 4cm/12 x 8 x 1½in baking tin (pan) with baking parchment and grease the paper.

2 With a sharp knife, chop the figs roughly. Set aside.

3 In a bowl, whisk the eggs and sugar until well blended. In another bowl, sift together the dry ingredients, then fold into the egg mixture in several batches.

4 Scrape the mixture into the baking tin and bake until the top is firm and brown, about 35–40 minutes. It should still be soft underneath.

5 Leave to cool in the tin for 5 minutes, then unmould and transfer to a sheet of baking parchment lightly sprinkled with icing sugar. Cut into bars.

> **Cook's Tip**
> Figs are healthy fruits containing calcium, iron and potassium. They also have antibacterial properties as well as being a laxative. Omit the brandy or cognac and these fig bars will make a good sweet to add to children's lunchboxes – but remember to add a paper napkin for those sticky fingers!

Lemon Bars

A surprising amount of lemon juice goes into these bars, but you will appreciate why when you taste them.

Makes 36
50g/2oz/½ cup icing
 (confectioners') sugar
175g/6oz/1½ cups plain
 (all-purpose) flour
2.5ml/½ tsp salt
175g/6oz/¾ cup butter, cut into
 small pieces

For the topping
4 eggs
350g/12oz/1¾ cups caster
 (superfine) sugar
grated rind of 1 lemon
120ml/4fl oz/½ cup fresh
 lemon juice
175ml/6fl oz/¾ cup
 whipping cream
icing (confectioners') sugar,
 for dusting

1 Preheat the oven to 160°C/325°F/Gas 3. Grease a 33 x 23cm/13 x 9in baking tin (pan).

2 Sift the sugar, flour and salt into a bowl. With a pastry blender, cut in the butter until the mixture resembles coarse breadcrumbs. Press the mixture into the base of the tin.

3 Bake until golden brown, about 20 minutes.

4 To make the topping, whisk the eggs and caster sugar together until well blended. Add the lemon rind and juice, and mix together well.

5 Lightly whip the cream and fold into the egg mixture. Pour over the still warm base, return to the oven, and bake until set, about 40 minutes. Cool completely before cutting into bars. Dust with icing sugar before serving.

> **Variation**
> Try orange in this recipe for a change. It will work just as well in the custard topping and will give the bars a delicately scented flavour.

Fig Bars Energy 53kcal/224kJ; Protein 1g; Carbohydrate 8.9g, of which sugars 7.7g; Fat 1.6g, of which saturates 0.2g; Cholesterol 12mg; Calcium 26mg; Fibre 0.7g; Sodium 9mg.
Lemon Bars Energy 124kcal/519kJ; Protein 1.3g; Carbohydrate 15.7g, of which sugars 12g; Fat 6.6g, of which saturates 3.9g; Cholesterol 37mg; Calcium 20mg; Fibre 0.2g; Sodium 39mg.

Spiced Raisin Bars

If you like raisins, these gloriously spicy bars are for you. Omit the walnuts if you prefer.

Makes 30

100g/3³⁄₄oz/scant 1 cup plain (all-purpose) flour
7.5ml/1¹⁄₂ tsp baking powder
5ml/1 tsp ground cinnamon
2.5ml/¹⁄₂ tsp freshly grated nutmeg
1.5ml/¹⁄₄ tsp ground cloves
1.5ml/¹⁄₄ tsp mixed (apple pie) spice
215g/7¹⁄₂oz/1¹⁄₂ cups raisins
115g/4oz/¹⁄₂ cup butter or margarine, at room temperature
90g/3¹⁄₂oz/¹⁄₂ cup caster (superfine) sugar
2 eggs
170g/5³⁄₄oz/scant ¹⁄₂ cup black treacle (molasses)
50g/2oz/¹⁄₂ cup chopped walnuts

1 Preheat the oven to 180°C/350°F/Gas 4. Line a 33 x 23cm/13 x 9in baking tin (pan) with baking parchment and lightly grease the paper.

2 Sift together the flour, baking powder and spices. Place the raisins in another bowl and toss with a few tablespoons of the flour mixture.

3 With an electric mixer, cream the butter or margarine and caster sugar together until light and fluffy. Beat in the eggs, one at a time, and then add the black treacle. Stir in the flour mixture, raisins and chopped walnuts.

4 Spread evenly in the baking tin. Bake until just set, about 15–18 minutes. Cool in the tin before cutting into squares.

Cook's Tips
• *If you are a real raisin fan, try to use Muscat raisins, as they have a rich and sweet quality.*
• *If you are making bars or cookies that contain nuts to serve to children always chop the nuts finely, as they can be a choking hazard. Although you can omit the nuts completely they are a good source of protein.*

Toffee Meringue Bars

Two deliciously contrasting layers complement each other beautifully in these easy-to-make bars.

Makes 12

50g/2oz/¹⁄₄ cup butter
215g/7¹⁄₂oz/scant 1¹⁄₄ cups soft dark brown sugar
1 egg
2.5ml/¹⁄₂ tsp vanilla extract
65g/2¹⁄₂oz/9 tbsp plain (all-purpose) flour
2.5ml/¹⁄₂ tsp salt
1.5ml/¹⁄₄ tsp freshly grated nutmeg

For the topping
1 egg white
1.5ml/¹⁄₄ tsp salt
15ml/1 tbsp golden (light corn) syrup
90g/3¹⁄₂oz/¹⁄₂ cup caster (superfine) sugar
50g/2oz/¹⁄₂ cup finely chopped walnuts

1 Combine the butter and brown sugar in a pan and heat until bubbling. Set aside to cool.

2 Preheat the oven to 180°C/350°F/Gas 4. Line the base and sides of a 20cm/8in square cake tin (pan) with baking parchment and grease the paper.

3 Beat the egg and vanilla extract into the cooled sugar mixture. Sift over the flour, salt and nutmeg and fold in. Spread into the base of the cake tin.

4 To make the topping, beat the egg white with the salt until it holds soft peaks. Beat in the golden syrup, then the sugar, and continue beating until the mixture holds stiff peaks. Fold in the nuts and spread on top of the base. Bake for 30 minutes. Cut into bars when completely cool.

Cook's Tip
For this recipe, and any recipe that uses a traditional meringue, it is important to use a large grease-free bowl for whisking egg whites. Also, always check that the whisk or beaters are completely clean, as traces of grease will stop the whites from achieving stiff peaks.

Spiced Raisin Bars Energy 102kcal/429kJ; Protein 1.2g; Carbohydrate 14.6g, of which sugars 12g; Fat 4.7g, of which saturates 2.2g; Cholesterol 21mg; Calcium 45mg; Fibre 0.3g; Sodium 43mg.
Meringue Bars Energy 189kcal/797kJ; Protein 2g; Carbohydrate 31.9g, of which sugars 27.8g; Fat 6.8g, of which saturates 2.5g; Cholesterol 25mg; Calcium 28mg; Fibre 0.3g; Sodium 42mg.

Oat and Date Brownies

These brownies are marvellous as a break-time treat. The secret of chewy, moist brownies is not to overcook them.

Makes 16
150g/5oz plain (semisweet)
    chocolate
50g/2oz/¼ cup butter
75g/3oz/scant 1 cup rolled oats
25g/1oz/3 tbsp wheatgerm
25g/1oz/⅓ cup milk powder
2.5ml/½ tsp baking powder
2.5ml/½ tsp salt
50g/2oz/½ cup chopped walnuts
50g/2oz/⅓ cup finely
    chopped dates
50g/2oz/¼ cup muscovado
    (molasses) sugar
5ml/1 tsp vanilla extract
2 eggs, beaten

1 Break the chocolate into a heatproof bowl and add the butter. Place over a pan of simmering water and stir until completely melted.

2 Cool the chocolate, stirring occasionally. Preheat the oven to 180°C/350°F/Gas 4. Grease and line a 20cm/8in square cake tin (pan).

3 Combine the oats, wheatgerm, milk powder and baking powder together in a bowl. Add the salt, walnuts, chopped dates and sugar, and mix well. Beat in the melted chocolate, vanilla and beaten eggs.

4 Pour the mixture into the cake tin, level the surface and bake in the oven for 20–25 minutes, or until firm around the edges yet still soft in the centre.

5 Cool the brownies in the tin, then chill in the refrigerator. When they are more solid, turn them out and cut into 16 squares.

Cook's Tip
When melting chocolate always make sure that the water in the pan does not touch the bowl, or it might bubble up the side of the bowl and splash into the chocolate, changing its texture.

Banana Chocolate Brownies

Nuts traditionally give brownies their chewy texture. Here oat bran is used instead, creating a wonderful alternative.

Makes 9
75ml/5 tbsp unsweetened
    cocoa powder
15ml/1 tbsp caster
    (superfine) sugar
75ml/5 tbsp milk
3 large bananas, mashed
215g/7½oz/scant 1 cup soft light
    brown sugar
5ml/1 tsp vanilla extract
5 egg whites
75g/3oz/⅔ cup self-raising
    (self-rising) flour
75g/3oz/⅔ cup oat bran
icing (confectioners') sugar,
    for dusting

1 Preheat the oven to 180°C/350°F/Gas 4. Line a 20cm/8in square cake tin (pan) with non-stick baking paper.

2 Blend the cocoa powder and caster sugar with the milk. Add the bananas, soft brown sugar and vanilla extract. Lightly beat the egg whites with a fork. Add the chocolate mixture and continue to beat well. Sift the flour over the mixture and fold in with the oat bran. Pour into the prepared tin.

3 Cook in the oven for 40 minutes, or until firm. Cool in the tin for 10 minutes, then turn out on to a wire rack. Cut into squares and lightly dust with icing sugar before serving.

Cook's Tips
Win a few brownie points by getting to know what makes them great.
• They should be moist and chewy with a sugary crust on the outside but squidgy on the inside.
• True versions contain a high proportion of sugar and fat and most contain nuts. Lighter versions often contain white chocolate and are often referred to as blondies.
• Brownies make superb individual cakes but the cooked slab can also be left whole and then served as a larger cake for dessert, decorated with cream and fruit.

Banana Gingerbread Slices

Bananas make this spicy bake delightfully moist and add a natural sweetness. The flavour develops on keeping, so store for a few days before cutting.

Makes 20 slices
275g/10oz/2¹/₂ cups plain (all-purpose) flour
20ml/4 tsp ground ginger
10ml/2 tsp mixed (apple pie) spice
5ml/1 tsp bicarbonate of soda (baking soda)
115g/4oz/¹/₂ cup soft light brown sugar
60ml/4 tbsp corn oil
30ml/2 tbsp molasses or black treacle
30ml/2 tbsp malt extract
2 eggs, beaten
60ml/4 tbsp orange juice
3 ripe bananas
115g/4oz/scant 1 cup raisins or sultanas (golden raisins)

1 Preheat the oven to 180°C/350°F/Gas 4. Line and grease a 28 x 18cm/11 x 7in baking tin (pan).

2 Sift the flour, ground ginger and mixed spice and the bicarbonate of soda into a mixing bowl. Spoon some of the mixture back into the sieve, add the brown sugar and sift the mixture back into the bowl.

3 Make a well in the centre of the dry ingredients and add the oil, molasses or treacle, malt extract, eggs, and orange juice. Gradually stir the dry ingredients into the liquid working from the centre outwards. Mix thoroughly.

4 Peel the bananas and mash them in a bowl. Add to the gingerbread mixture with the raisins or sultanas. Mix the ingredients thoroughly to combine well.

5 Scrape the mixture into the prepared tin. Bake for 35–40 minutes, or until the centre springs back when the surface of the cake is lightly pressed.

6 Leave the gingerbread in the tin to cool for 5 minutes, then turn on to a wire rack, remove the lining paper and leave to cool completely. Serve spread with butter, if you like.

Spiced Date and Walnut Cake

Nuts and dates are a classic flavour combination. Use pecan nuts instead of walnuts, if you wish.

Makes one 900g/2lb cake
300g/11oz/2²/₃ cups self-raising (self-rising) wholemeal (whole-wheat) flour
10ml/2 tsp mixed (apple pie) spice
150g/5oz/³/₄ cup chopped dates
50g/2oz/¹/₂ cup chopped walnuts
60ml/4 tbsp sunflower oil
115g/4oz/¹/₂ cup dark muscovado (molasses) sugar
300ml/¹/₂ pint/1¹/₄ cups milk
walnut halves, to decorate

1 Preheat the oven to 180°C/350°F/Gas 4. Line a 900g/2lb loaf tin (pan) with baking parchment and grease the paper.

2 Sift together the flour and spice, adding back any bran from the sieve. Stir in the dates and walnuts.

3 Mix the oil, sugar and milk in a separate bowl. Add the oil mixture to the dry ingredients and mix to combine thoroughly.

4 Spoon the cake mixture into the prepared loaf tin and arrange the walnut halves on top.

5 Bake the cake in the oven for about 45–50 minutes, or until it is golden brown and firm.

6 Turn out the cake, remove the lining paper, and leave to cool on a wire rack.

> **Cook's Tip**
> Dried fruits add natural sweetness as well as moisture to baking. Always chop dried fruits by hand, as a food processor will chop them too finely. Dates bought in a block are ideal for cooking as they have no stones (pits) and you can use a sharp knife to slice horizontally through the block in thin slices. The slices can then easily be broken up into small pieces and chopped smaller if you prefer.

Slices Energy 132kcal/556kJ; Protein 2.3g; Carbohydrate 25.4g, of which sugars 14.6g; Fat 3g, of which saturates 0.5g; Cholesterol 19mg; Calcium 37mg; Fibre 0.7g; Sodium 14mg.
Cake Energy 2666kcal/11243kJ; Protein 61.2g; Carbohydrate 429.6g, of which sugars 243.9g; Fat 90.2g, of which saturates 12.3g; Cholesterol 18mg; Calcium 649mg; Fibre 34.8g; Sodium 163mg.

Sweet Potato and Raisin Bread

Serve buttered slices of this subtly spiced loaf at coffee or tea time.

Makes one 900g/2lb loaf
350g/12oz/3 cups plain
   (all-purpose) flour
10ml/2 tsp baking powder
2.5ml/½ tsp salt
5ml/1 tsp ground cinnamon
2.5ml/½ tsp freshly grated nutmeg
450g/1lb mashed cooked
   sweet potatoes
90g/3½oz/½ cup soft light
   brown sugar
115g/4oz/½ cup butter
   or margarine, melted
   and cooled
3 eggs, beaten
75g/3oz/generous ½ cup raisins

1 Preheat the oven to 180°C/350°F/Gas 4. Grease a 900g/2lb loaf dish or tin (pan).

2 Sift the flour, baking powder, salt, cinnamon, and nutmeg into a small bowl. Set aside.

3 With an electric mixer, beat the mashed sweet potatoes with the brown sugar, butter or margarine, and eggs until well mixed.

4 Add the flour mixture and the raisins. Stir with a wooden spoon until the flour is just mixed in.

5 Transfer the batter to the prepared dish or tin. Bake until a skewer inserted in the centre of the loaf comes out clean, about 1–1¼ hours.

6 Let the bread cool in the pan on a wire rack for 15 minutes, then unmould from the dish or tin on to the wire rack and leave to cool completely.

Cook's Tip
Soft light and dark brown sugars are both comprised of white sugar with added molasses, which gives them a moist and delicate flavour. Soft dark brown sugar has more molasses added to give it a richer colour and more intense flavour.

Lemon and Walnut Teabread

Beaten egg whites give this citrus-flavour loaf a lovely light and crumbly texture.

Makes one 23 x 13cm/ 9 x 5in loaf
115g/4oz/½ cup butter or
   margarine, at room temperature
90g/3½oz/½ cup caster
   (superfine) sugar
2 eggs, at room temperature,
   separated
grated rind of 2 lemons
30ml/2 tbsp lemon juice
215g/7½oz/scant 2 cups plain
   (all-purpose) flour
10ml/2 tsp baking powder
120ml/4fl oz/½ cup milk
50g/2oz/½ cup chopped walnuts
1.5ml/¼ tsp salt

1 Preheat the oven to 180°C/350°F/Gas 4. Then line a 23 x 13cm/9 x 5in loaf tin (pan) with baking parchment and grease the paper.

2 Cream the butter or margarine with the sugar until light and fluffy. Beat in the egg yolks. Add the lemon rind and juice, and stir until blended. Set aside.

3 In another bowl, sift together the flour and baking powder three times. Fold into the butter mixture in three batches, alternating with the milk. Fold in the walnuts. Set aside.

4 Beat the egg whites and salt until stiff peaks form. Fold a large spoonful of the egg whites into the walnut mixture to lighten it. Fold in the remaining egg whites carefully until the mixture is just blended.

5 Pour the batter into the prepared tin and bake until a skewer inserted in the centre of the loaf comes out clean, about 45–50 minutes. Cool in the tin for 5 minutes before turning out on to a wire rack to cool completely.

Cook's Tip
Make sure that there is no egg yolk in the white or it will stop it from whisking up properly.

Sweet Sesame Loaf

Lemon and sesame seeds make a great partnership in this light teabread.

Makes one 23 x 13cm/ 9 x 5in loaf

75g/3oz/6 tbsp sesame seeds
275g/10oz/2½ cups plain (all-purpose) flour
12.5ml/2½ tsp baking powder
5ml/1 tsp salt
50g/2oz/¼ cup butter or margarine, at room temperature
130g/4½oz/scant ¾ cup caster (superfine) sugar
2 eggs, at room temperature
grated rind of 1 lemon
350ml/12fl oz/1½ cups milk

1 Preheat the oven to 180°C/350°F/Gas 4. Carefully line a 23 x 13cm/9 x 5in loaf tin (pan) with baking parchment and then grease the paper.

2 Reserve 25g/1oz/2 tbsp of the sesame seeds. Spread the rest on a baking sheet and bake in the oven until lightly toasted, about 10 minutes.

3 Sift the flour, baking powder and salt into a bowl. Stir in the toasted sesame seeds and set aside.

4 Cream the butter or margarine and sugar together until light and fluffy. Beat in the eggs, then stir in the lemon rind and milk. Pour the milk mixture over the dry ingredients and fold in with a large metal spoon until just blended.

5 Pour into the tin and sprinkle over the reserved sesame seeds. Bake until a skewer inserted in the centre comes out clean, about 1 hour. Cool in the tin for 10 minutes. Turn out on to a wire rack to cool completely.

> **Cook's Tip**
> *Sesame seeds are nutty flavoured and slightly sweet. Their flavour is enhanced by light toasting in a dry pan. However, because of their high oil content they do not store well and so you should always buy them in small quantities.*

Cardamom and Saffron Tea Loaf

An aromatic sweet bread ideal for afternoon tea, or lightly toasted for breakfast. The delicate spices of cardamom and saffron give it an unusual flavour.

Makes one 900g/2lb loaf

a generous pinch of saffron threads
750ml/1¼ pints/3 cups lukewarm milk
25g/1oz/2 tbsp butter
1kg/2¼lb/9 cups strong white bread flour
2 sachets easy-blend (rapid-rise) dried yeast
40g/1½oz/generous ¼ cup caster (superfine) sugar
6 cardamom pods, split open and seeds extracted
115g/4oz/scant ¾ cup raisins
30ml/2 tbsp clear honey, plus extra for glazing
1 egg, beaten

1 Crush the saffron straight into a cup containing a little of the warm milk and leave to infuse (steep) for 5 minutes.

2 Rub the butter into the flour using your fingertips or a pastry cutter, then mix in the yeast, sugar, cardamom seeds and raisins.

3 Beat the remaining milk with the honey and egg, then mix this into the flour, along with the saffron milk and threads, until the mixture forms a firm dough. Turn out the dough and knead it on a lightly floured surface for 5 minutes.

4 Return the dough to the mixing bowl, cover with oiled clear film (plastic wrap) and leave in a warm place until doubled in size.

5 Preheat the oven to 200°C/400°F/Gas 6. Grease a 900g/2lb loaf tin (pan). Turn the dough out on to a floured surface, knock back (punch down) and knead for 3 minutes.

6 Shape the dough into a fat roll and fit into the tin. Cover with a sheet of lightly oiled clear film and leave to stand in a warm place until the dough begins to rise again.

7 Bake the loaf for 25 minutes, or until golden brown and firm on top. Turn out on to a wire rack and as it cools brush the top with clear honey.

Sweet Sesame Energy 1691kcal/7142kJ; Protein 56g; Carbohydrate 283.8g, of which sugars 7.5g; Fat 44.7g, of which saturates 6.4g; Cholesterol 0mg; Calcium 793mg; Fibre 29.3g; Sodium 3955mg.
Saffron Loaf Energy 4571kcal/19407kJ; Protein 128.6g; Carbohydrate 956.8g, of which sugars 194.8g; Fat 52.3g, of which saturates 24.6g; Cholesterol 288mg; Calcium 2409mg; Fibre 33.3g; Sodium 649mg.

Banana and Cardamom Bread

The combination of banana and fragrant cardamom is delicious in this soft-textured moist loaf.

Serves 6
10 cardamom pods
400g/14oz/3½ cups strong white bread flour
5ml/1 tsp salt
5ml/1 tsp easy-blend (rapid-rise) dried yeast
150ml/¼ pint/⅔ cup hand-hot water
30ml/2 tbsp malt extract
2 ripe bananas, mashed
5ml/1 tsp sesame seeds

1 Grease a 450g/1lb loaf tin (pan). Split the cardamom pods, and remove the seeds and then chop the pods finely.

2 Sift the flour and salt into a large bowl, add the yeast and make a well in the centre. Add the water with the malt extract, chopped cardamom pods and bananas. Stir from the centre outwards, gradually incorporating the flour and mixing to a soft dough, and adding a little extra water if necessary.

3 Turn the dough on to a floured surface and knead for 5 minutes until smooth and elastic. Shape into a braid and place in the prepared tin. Cover loosely with clear film (plastic wrap) (ballooning it to trap the air) and leave in a warm place until well risen, about 1½ hours. Meanwhile, preheat the oven to 220°C/425°F/Gas 7.

4 Brush the braid lightly with water and sprinkle with the sesame seeds. Bake for 10 minutes, then lower the oven temperature to 200°C/400°F/Gas 6. Cook for 15 minutes more, or until the loaf sounds hollow when tapped underneath. Remove to a wire rack to cool.

> **Cook's Tip**
> *Cardamom is a green or white seed pod containing tiny black seeds. It has a distinctive warm and pronounced scent that really works well in cakes, pastries and desserts.*

Swedish Sultana Bread

A lightly sweetened bread that goes very well with a selection of cheeses and that is also excellent toasted at teatime.

Serves 10
225g/8oz/2 cups strong wholemeal (whole-wheat) bread flour
225g/8oz/2 cups strong white bread flour
5ml/1 tsp easy-blend (rapid-rise) dried yeast
5ml/1 tsp salt
115g/4oz/⅔ cup sultanas (golden raisins)
50g/2oz/½ cup walnuts, chopped
15ml/1 tbsp clear honey
150ml/¼ pint/⅔ cup hand-hot water
175ml/6fl oz/¾ cup hand-hot skimmed milk, plus extra for glazing

1 Grease a baking sheet. Put the flours in a bowl with the yeast, salt and sultanas.

2 Set aside 15ml/1 tbsp of the walnuts and add the remainder to the bowl. Mix the ingredients lightly and make a well in the centre.

3 Dissolve the honey in the water and add the mixture to the bowl with the milk. Stir from the centre outwards, gradually incorporating the flour, and mixing to a soft dough, and adding a little extra water if necessary.

4 Turn the dough on to a floured surface and knead for 5 minutes, or until smooth and elastic. Shape into a 28cm/11in long sausage shape. Place on the prepared baking sheet.

5 Make diagonal cuts down the length of the loaf. Brush the top with milk, sprinkle with the remaining walnuts and leave in a warm place until doubled in size, about 1½ hours. Meanwhile, preheat the oven to 220°C/425°F/Gas 7.

6 Bake the loaf for 10 minutes, then lower the oven temperature to 200°C/400°F/Gas 6 and bake for 20 minutes more or until the loaf sounds hollow when tapped underneath. Remove to a wire rack to cool.

Cardamom Bread Energy 279kcal/1185kJ; Protein 6.8g; Carbohydrate 63.5g, of which sugars 11.9g; Fat 1.5g, of which saturates 0.2g; Cholesterol 0mg; Calcium 102mg; Fibre 2.5g; Sodium 16mg.
Sultana Bread Energy 225kcal/953kJ; Protein 5.9g; Carbohydrate 43.9g, of which sugars 9.6g; Fat 4.1g, of which saturates 0.4g; Cholesterol 1mg; Calcium 96mg; Fibre 1.8g; Sodium 12mg.

Prune Bread

Moist inside, with a crusty walnut topping.

Makes 1 loaf
225g/8oz/1 cup prunes
15ml/1 tbsp active dried yeast
75g/3oz/²⁄₃ cup strong wholemeal (whole-wheat) bread flour
400–425g/14–15oz/3½–3²⁄₃ cups strong white bread flour
2.5ml/½ tsp bicarbonate of soda (baking soda)
5ml/1 tsp salt
5ml/1 tsp pepper
25g/1oz/2 tbsp butter, at room temperature
175ml/6fl oz/³⁄₄ cup buttermilk
50g/2oz/½ cup walnuts, chopped
milk, for glazing

1 Simmer the prunes in water to cover until soft, about 20 minutes, or soak overnight. Drain, reserving 60ml/4 tbsp of the soaking liquid. Pit and chop the prunes.

2 Combine the yeast and the reserved prune liquid, stir and leave for 15 minutes to dissolve and so that the yeast becomes frothy.

3 In a large bowl, stir together the wholemeal and white flours, bicarbonate of soda, salt and pepper. Make a well in the centre. Add the prunes, butter and buttermilk. Pour in the yeast mixture. With a wooden spoon, stir from the centre, folding in more flour with each turn, to obtain a rough dough.

4 Transfer to a floured surface and knead until smooth and elastic. This will take about 10 minutes. Return to the bowl, cover with clear film (plastic wrap) and leave to rise in a warm place until doubled in volume, about 1½ hours. Grease a baking sheet.

5 Knock back (punch down) the dough with your fist, then knead in the walnuts. Shape the dough into a long, cylindrical loaf. Place on the baking sheet, cover loosely, and leave to rise in a warm place for 45 minutes. Preheat the oven to 220°C/425°F/Gas 7. With a sharp knife, score the top. Brush with milk and bake for 15 minutes. Lower to 190°C/375°F/Gas 5 and bake for 35 minutes more, or until the base sounds hollow. Cool.

Malt Loaf

This is a rich and sticky loaf. If it lasts long enough to go stale, try toasting it for a delicious teatime treat.

Serves 8
350g/12oz/3 cups strong white bread flour
1.5ml/¼ tsp salt
5ml/1 tsp easy-blend (rapid-rise) dried yeast
a pinch of caster (superfine) sugar
30ml/2 tbsp soft light brown sugar
175g/6oz/1 cup sultanas (golden raisins)
150ml/¼ pint/²⁄₃ cup hand-hot skimmed milk
15ml/1 tbsp sunflower oil
45ml/3 tbsp malt extract

To glaze
30ml/2 tbsp caster (superfine) sugar
30ml/2 tbsp water

1 Sift the flour and salt into a mixing bowl, and stir in the yeast, the pinch of sugar, brown sugar and sultanas.

2 Make a well in the centre of the dry ingredients. Add the hot milk with the oil and malt extract. Stir from the centre outwards, gradually incorporating the flour and mixing to a soft dough, and adding a little extra milk if necessary.

3 Turn on to a floured surface and knead for about 5 minutes until smooth and elastic. Lightly oil a 450g/1lb loaf tin (pan).

4 Shape the dough and place it in the prepared tin. Cover with a damp dish cloth or some oiled clear film (plastic wrap) and leave in a warm place until doubled in size, about 1½ hours. Meanwhile, preheat the oven to 190°C/375°F/Gas 5.

5 Bake the loaf for 30–35 minutes, or until it sounds hollow when tapped underneath.

6 While the loaf is baking, make the glaze by dissolving the sugar in the water in a small pan. Bring to the boil, stirring, then lower the heat and simmer for 1 minute.

7 Brush the loaf while hot, then transfer it to a wire rack to cool.

Malt Loaf Energy 259kcal/1101kJ; Protein 5.4g; Carbohydrate 58.4g, of which sugars 25g; Fat 2.1g, of which saturates 0.3g; Cholesterol 1mg; Calcium 101mg; Fibre 1.8g; Sodium 29mg.
Prune Bread Energy 2520kcal/10639kJ; Protein 65.6g; Carbohydrate 433.3g, of which sugars 93.2g; Fat 70.4g, of which saturates 19.9g; Cholesterol 70mg; Calcium 915mg; Fibre 33.4g; Sodium 2266mg.

Pear and Sultana Teabread

This is an ideal teabread to make when pears are plentiful. There's no better use for autumn windfalls.

Serves 6 – 8

25g/1oz/3 cups rolled oats
50g/2oz/¼ cup soft light
  brown sugar
30ml/2 tbsp pear or apple juice
30ml/2 tbsp sunflower oil
1 large or 2 small ripe pears
115g/4oz/1 cup self-raising
  (self-rising) flour
115g/4oz/¾ cup sultanas
  (golden raisins)
2.5ml/½ tsp baking powder
10ml/2 tsp mixed (apple
  pie) spice
1 egg

1 Preheat the oven to 180°C/350°F/Gas 4. Line a 450g/1lb loaf tin (pan) with baking parchment.

2 Put the oats in a bowl with the sugar, and pour over the pear or apple juice and oil.

3 Mix the ingredients together well using a wooden spoon or electric whisk. Leave to stand for 15 minutes.

4 Quarter, core and grate the pear(s). Add to the bowl with the flour, sultanas, baking powder, spice and egg. Using a wooden spoon, mix thoroughly.

5 Spoon the teabread mixture into the prepared loaf tin. Bake for 55–60 minutes, or until a skewer inserted into the centre comes out clean.

6 Invert the teabread on a wire rack and remove the lining paper. Leave to cool.

Cook's Tips
• Health-food stores sell concentrated pear juice, ready for diluting as required.
• You will also find some good-quality sultanas there and organic oats if you want to make a really healthy treat.

Banana and Ginger Teabread

The creaminess of the banana is given a delightful lift with chunks of stem ginger in this tasty teabread. If you like a strong ginger flavour add 5ml/1 tsp ground ginger with the flour.

Serves 6 – 8

175g/6oz/1½ cups self-raising
  (self-rising) flour
5ml/1 tsp baking powder
40g/1½oz/3 tbsp soft margarine
50g/2oz/¼ cup soft light
  brown sugar
50g/2oz/⅓ cup drained
  preserved stem ginger, chopped
60ml/4 tbsp skimmed milk
2 ripe bananas

1 Preheat the oven to 180°C/350°F/Gas 4. Line and grease a 450g/1lb loaf tin (pan).

2 Sift the flour and baking powder into a large bowl.

3 Using your fingertips or a pastry cutter rub the margarine into the dry ingredients until the mixture resembles breadcrumbs, then stir in the sugar.

4 Peel and mash the bananas in a separate bowl.

5 Add the preserved stem ginger, milk and mashed bananas to the mixture and mix to a soft dough. Spoon into the prepared tin and bake for 40–45 minutes.

6 Run a metal spatula around the edges of the cake to loosen them, then turn the teabread on to a wire rack and leave to cool completely.

Variation
To make Banana and Walnut Teabread, add 5ml/1 tsp mixed (apple pie) spice and omit the chopped stem ginger. Stir in 50g/2oz/½ cup chopped walnuts and add 50g/2oz/⅓ cup sultanas (golden raisins).

Pear and Sultana Energy 184kcal/780kJ; Protein 3.1g; Carbohydrate 36.3g, of which sugars 23.1g; Fat 4g, of which saturates 0.6g; Cholesterol 24mg; Calcium 43mg; Fibre 1.8g; Sodium 16mg.
Banana and Ginger Energy 162kcal/685kJ; Protein 2.7g; Carbohydrate 29.7g, of which sugars 12.5g; Fat 4.5g, of which saturates 0.1g; Cholesterol 0mg; Calcium 45mg; Fibre 1g; Sodium 45mg.

Wholemeal Banana Nut Loaf

A hearty and filling loaf, this would be ideal as a winter tea-time treat.

Makes one 23 x 13cm/ 9 x 5in loaf

115g/4oz/½ cup butter, at room temperature

115g/4oz/generous ½ cup caster (superfine) sugar

2 eggs, at room temperature

115g/4oz/1 cup plain (all-purpose) flour

5ml/1 tsp bicarbonate of soda (baking soda)

1.5ml/¼ tsp salt

5ml/1 tsp ground cinnamon

50g/2oz/½ cup wholemeal (whole-wheat) flour

3 large ripe bananas

5ml/1 tsp vanilla extract

50g/2oz/½ cup chopped walnuts

1 Preheat the oven to 180°C/350°F/Gas 4. Line the base and sides of a 23 x 13cm/9 x 5in loaf tin (pan) with baking parchment and grease the paper.

2 With an electric mixer, cream the butter and sugar together until light and fluffy. Add the eggs, one at a time, beating well after each addition.

3 Sift the plain flour, bicarbonate of soda, salt and cinnamon over the butter mixture, and stir to blend. Then stir in the wholemeal flour.

4 With a fork, mash the bananas to a purée, then stir into the mixture. Stir in the vanilla and nuts.

5 Pour the mixture into the prepared tin and spread level. Bake until a skewer inserted in the centre comes out clean, about 50–60 minutes. Leave to stand for 10 minutes before transferring to a wire rack to cool completely.

> **Cook's Tip**
> *Wholemeal (whole-wheat) flour contains the wheat germ and bran, giving it a higher fibre, fat and nutritional content than white flour. Because of its fat content it is best stored in a cool larder.*

Apricot Nut Loaf

Raisins and walnuts combine with apricots to make a lovely light teabread. Full of flavour, it is also ideal for a morning snack or children's lunchboxes.

Makes one 23 x 13cm/ 9 x 5in loaf

115g/4oz/½ cup ready-to-eat dried apricots

1 large orange

75g/3oz/generous ½ cup raisins

150g/5oz/¾ cup caster (superfine) sugar

85ml/5½ tbsp/⅓ cup oil

2 eggs, lightly beaten

250g/9oz/2¼ cups plain (all-purpose) flour

10ml/2 tsp baking powder

2.5ml/½ tsp salt

5ml/1 tsp bicarbonate of soda (baking soda)

50g/2oz/½ cup chopped walnuts

1 Place the apricots in a bowl, cover with lukewarm water and leave to stand for 30 minutes. Preheat the oven to 180°C/350°F/Gas 4. Line a 23 x 13cm/9 x 5in loaf tin (pan) with baking parchment and grease the paper.

2 With a vegetable peeler, remove the orange rind, leaving the pith. Chop the strips finely.

3 Drain the softened apricots and chop them coarsely. Place in a bowl with the orange rind and raisins. Squeeze the peeled orange over a bowl. Measure the orange juice and add enough hot water to obtain 175ml/6fl oz/¾ cup liquid.

4 Add the orange juice mixture to the apricot mixture. Stir in the sugar, oil and eggs. Set aside.

5 In another bowl, sift together the flour, baking powder, salt and bicarbonate of soda. Fold the flour mixture into the apricot mixture in three batches, then stir in the walnuts.

6 Spoon the mixture into the prepared tin and bake until a skewer inserted in the centre of the loaf comes out clean, about 55–60 minutes. If the loaf browns too quickly, protect the top with a sheet of foil. Cool in the tin for 10 minutes, then transfer to a wire rack to cool completely.

Banana Energy 2632kcal/11017kJ; Protein 41.9g; Carbohydrate 313.4g, of which sugars 187.6g; Fat 143.4g, of which saturates 66.5g; Cholesterol 626mg; Calcium 384mg; Fibre 13.1g; Sodium 855mg.
Apricot Energy 2904kcal/12229kJ; Protein 51.6g; Carbohydrate 456.8g, of which sugars 265.9g; Fat 109.6g, of which saturates 13.6g; Cholesterol 381mg; Calcium 708mg; Fibre 20.3g; Sodium 227mg.

Orange and Honey Teabread

Honey gives a special flavour to this teabread. Serve just with a scraping of butter.

**Makes one 23 x 13cm/
9 x 5in loaf**

385g/13½oz/scant 3½ cups plain (all-purpose) flour
12.5ml/2½ tsp baking powder
2.5ml/½ tsp bicarbonate of soda (baking soda)
2.5ml/½ tsp salt
25g/1oz/2 tbsp margarine
250ml/8fl oz/1 cup clear honey
1 egg, at room temperature, lightly beaten
25ml/1½ tbsp grated orange rind
175ml/6fl oz/¾ cup freshly squeezed orange juice
115g/4oz/1 cup chopped walnuts

1 Preheat the oven to 160°C/325°F/Gas 3. Line the base and sides of a 23 x 13cm/9 x 5in loaf tin (pan) with baking parchment and grease the paper.

2 Sift the flour, baking powder, bicarbonate of soda and salt together in a bowl.

3 Cream the margarine until soft. Stir in the honey until blended, then stir in the egg. Add the orange rind and combine well.

4 Fold the flour mixture into the honey mixture in three batches, alternating with the orange juice. Stir in the walnuts.

5 Pour into the prepared tin and bake in the oven until a skewer inserted in the centre comes out clean, about 60–70 minutes. Leave for 10 minutes before turning out on to a wire rack to cool completely.

Cook's Tip
Although you can buy beautifully scented honey with the fragrance of wild flowers and herbs, the scents are usually destroyed in cooking, so for recipes such as this a less expensive honey will do perfectly well. Clear honey gradually becomes cloudy, but this can be rectified simply by gently heating it.

Apple Loaf

The apple sauce in this loaf makes it beautifully moist – it tastes perfect simply sliced and spread with butter.

**Makes one 23 x 13cm/
9 x 5in loaf**

1 egg
250ml/8fl oz/1 cup bottled or home-made apple sauce
50g/2oz/¼ cup butter or margarine, melted
100g/3¾oz/scant ½ cup soft dark brown sugar
45g/1¾oz/scant ¼ cup caster (superfine) sugar
275g/10oz/2½ cups plain (all-purpose) flour
10ml/2 tsp baking powder
2.5ml/½ tsp bicarbonate of soda (baking soda)
2.5ml/½ tsp salt
5ml/1 tsp ground cinnamon
2.5ml/½ tsp freshly grated nutmeg
65g/2½oz/½ cup currants or raisins
50g/2oz/½ cup pecan nuts or walnuts, chopped

1 Preheat the oven to 180°C/350°F/Gas 4. Line the base and sides of a 23 x 13cm/9 x 5in loaf tin (pan) with baking parchment and grease the paper.

2 Break the egg into a bowl and beat lightly. Stir in the apple sauce, butter or margarine, and both sugars. Set aside.

3 In another bowl, sift together the flour, baking powder, bicarbonate of soda, salt, cinnamon and nutmeg. Fold the dry ingredients, including the currants or raisins and the nuts, into the apple sauce mixture in three batches.

4 Pour into the prepared tin and bake in the oven until a skewer inserted in the centre of the loaf comes out clean, about 1 hour. Leave to stand in the tin for 10 minutes, then turn out on to a wire rack to cool completely.

Variations
Ring the changes with this moist loaf by using different nuts and dried fruit. Try ready-to-eat dried apricots with hazelnuts, for example.

Teabread Energy 3145kcal/13251kJ; Protein 61.3g; Carbohydrate 509.6g, of which sugars 215.4g; Fat 109.9g, of which saturates 8.8g; Cholesterol 190mg; Calcium 707mg; Fibre 16.1g; Sodium 335mg.
Apple Loaf Energy 2558kcal/10777kJ; Protein 42.6g; Carbohydrate 432.4g, of which sugars 222.5g; Fat 85g, of which saturates 30.9g; Cholesterol 297mg; Calcium 586mg; Fibre 15.3g; Sodium 442mg.

Date and Nut Malt Loaf

Choose any type of nut you like to include in this deliciously rich and fruit-packed teabread.

Makes two 450g/1lb loaves
300g/11oz/2⅔ cups strong plain
   (all-purpose) flour
275g/10oz/2½ cups strong
   wholemeal (whole-wheat)
   bread flour
5ml/1 tsp salt
75g/3oz/⅓ cup soft light
   brown sugar
1 sachet easy-blend (rapid-rise)
   dried yeast
50g/2oz/¼ cup butter
   or margarine
15ml/1 tbsp black treacle (molasses)
60ml/4 tbsp malt extract
scant 250ml/8fl oz/1 cup
   lukewarm milk
115g/4oz/⅔ cup chopped dates
75g/3oz/½ cup sultanas
   (golden raisins)
50g/2oz/½ cup chopped nuts
75g/3oz/generous ½ cup raisins
30ml/2 tbsp clear honey, to glaze

1 Sift the flours and salt into a large bowl, then tip in the wheat flakes from the sieve. Stir in the sugar and yeast.

2 Put the butter or margarine in a small pan with the treacle and malt extract. Stir over a low heat until melted. Leave to cool, then combine with the milk.

3 Stir the milk mixture into the dry ingredients and knead thoroughly for 15 minutes, or until the dough is elastic.

4 Knead in the chopped dates, sultanas and chopped nuts. Transfer the dough to an oiled bowl, cover with clear film (plastic wrap) and leave in a warm place for about 1½ hours, or until the dough has doubled in size.

5 Grease two 450g/1lb loaf tins (pans). Knock back (punch down) the dough and knead lightly. Divide the dough in half, form into loaves and place in the tins. Cover and leave in a warm place for 30 minutes, or until risen. Meanwhile, preheat the oven to 190°C/375°F/Gas 5.

6 Bake for 35–40 minutes, or until well risen. Cool on a wire rack. Brush with honey while warm.

Orange Wheatloaf

Perfect just with butter as a breakfast teabread, and for banana sandwiches.

Makes one 450g/1lb loaf
275g/10oz/2½ cups plain
   (all-purpose) wholemeal
   (whole-wheat) flour
2.5ml/½ tsp salt
25g/1oz/2 tbsp butter
25g/1oz/2 tbsp soft light
   brown sugar
½ sachet easy-blend (rapid-rise)
   dried yeast
grated rind and juice of
   ½ orange

1 Lightly grease a 450g/1lb loaf tin (pan). Sift the flour into a large bowl and add any wheat flakes from the sieve to the flour. Add the salt and rub in the butter lightly with your fingertips or a pastry cutter.

2 Stir in the sugar, yeast and orange rind. Pour the orange juice into a measuring jug and use hot water to make up to 200ml/7fl oz/scant 1 cup (the liquid should not be more than hand hot).

3 Stir the liquid into the flour mixture and mix to a soft ball of dough. Knead gently on a lightly floured surface until quite smooth and elastic.

4 Place the dough in the tin and leave it in a warm place until nearly doubled in size. Preheat the oven to 220°C/425°F/Gas 7.

5 Bake the bread for 30–35 minutes, or until it sounds hollow when removed from the tin and tapped underneath. Tip out of the tin and cool on a wire rack.

> **Cook's Tip**
> Easy-blend (rapid-rise) yeast is mixed directly with the dry ingredients and is the easiest yeast to use. Don't confuse this with active dried yeast, which needs to be mixed with liquid first and left to become frothy before it is mixed with the dry ingredients.

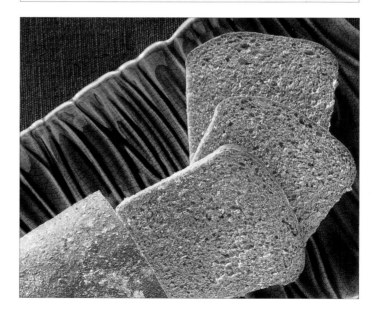

Malt Loaf Energy 1939kcal/8200kJ; Protein 43.9g; Carbohydrate 361.7g, of which sugars 162.2g; Fat 45.2g, of which saturates 16.6g; Cholesterol 61mg; Calcium 693mg; Fibre 21.7g; Sodium 308mg.
Wheatloaf Energy 1146kcal/4848kJ; Protein 35.3g; Carbohydrate 204.2g, of which sugars 34.3g; Fat 26.6g, of which saturates 13.8g; Cholesterol 53mg; Calcium 125mg; Fibre 24.8g; Sodium 164mg.

Banana Orange Loaf

For the best banana flavour and a really good, moist texture, make sure that the bananas are perfectly ripe for this cake.

Makes one 23 x 13cm/ 9 x 5in loaf

90g/3¹/₂oz/³/₄ cup plain (all-purpose) wholemeal (whole-wheat) flour
90g/3¹/₂oz/³/₄ cup plain (all-purpose) flour
5ml/1 tsp baking powder
5ml/1 tsp mixed (apple pie) spice
45ml/3 tbsp flaked (sliced) hazelnuts, toasted
2 large ripe bananas
1 egg
30ml/2 tbsp sunflower oil
30ml/2 tbsp clear honey
finely grated rind and juice of 1 small orange
4 orange slices, halved
10ml/2 tsp icing (confectioners') sugar

1 Preheat the oven to 180°C/350°F/Gas 4. Brush a 23 x 13cm/ 9 x 5in loaf tin (pan) with sunflower oil and line the base with baking parchment.

2 Sift the flours with the baking powder and spice into a large bowl, adding any bran that is caught in the sieve (strainer). Stir the hazelnuts into the dry ingredients.

3 Peel and mash the bananas in a large bowl. Add the egg, sunflower oil, honey, and the orange rind and juice to the mashed bananas and beat together.

4 Add the banana mixture to the dry ingredients and mix to combine thoroughly.

5 Spoon the mixture into the prepared tin and smooth the top. Bake in the oven for 40–45 minutes, or until the cake is firm and golden brown. Remove from the oven and turn out on to a wire rack to cool.

6 Meanwhile, sprinkle the orange slices with the icing sugar and place on a grill (broiling) rack. Grill until lightly golden. Arrange the glazed orange slices on the top of the loaf.

Banana Bread

For a change, add 50–75g/ 2–3oz/¹/₂–³/₄ cup chopped walnuts or pecan nuts with the dry ingredients.

Makes one 21 x 12cm/ 8¹/₂ x 4¹/₂in loaf

200g/7oz/1²/₃ cups plain (all-purpose) flour
11.5ml/2¹/₄ tsp baking powder
2.5ml/¹/₂ tsp salt
4ml/³/₄ tsp ground cinnamon (optional)
60ml/4 tbsp wheatgerm
65g/2¹/₂oz/5 tbsp butter, at room temperature
115g/4oz/generous ¹/₂ cup caster (superfine) sugar
4ml/³/₄ tsp grated lemon rind
3 ripe bananas, mashed
2 eggs, beaten

1 Preheat the oven to 180°C/350°F/Gas 4. Grease and flour a 21 x 12cm/8¹/₂ x 4¹/₂in loaf tin (pan).

2 Sift the flour, baking powder, salt and cinnamon, if using, into a bowl. Stir in the wheatgerm.

3 In another bowl, combine the butter with the caster sugar and grated lemon rind. Beat thoroughly until the mixture is light and fluffy.

4 Add the mashed bananas and eggs, and mix well. Add the dry ingredients and blend quickly and evenly.

5 Spoon into the loaf tin. Bake for 50–60 minutes, or until a skewer inserted in the centre comes out clean.

6 Cool the bread in the tin for 5 minutes, then turn out on to a wire rack to cool completely.

Cook's Tip
Wheatgerm is the heart of the wheat grain and contains many nutrients and important vitamins. It must be used fresh and should be stored in an airtight container. Do not store for long periods, as it will become bitter.

Bread Energy 2265kcal/9548kJ; Protein 51.9g; Carbohydrate 372.4g, of which sugars 195.9g; Fat 73.6g, of which saturates 38.4g; Cholesterol 519mg; Calcium 461mg; Fibre 18.9g; Sodium 553mg.
Loaf Energy 1483kcal/6238kJ; Protein 35.3g; Carbohydrate 214.3g, of which sugars 84.6g; Fat 59.9g, of which saturates 7g; Cholesterol 190mg; Calcium 276mg; Fibre 16.1g; Sodium 89mg.

Marmalade Teabread

If you prefer, leave the top of the loaf plain and serve sliced and lightly buttered instead.

Makes one 21 x 12cm/ 8½ x 4½in loaf

200g/7oz/1⅔ cups plain (all-purpose) flour
5ml/1 tsp baking powder
6.5ml/1¼ tsp ground cinnamon
90g/3½oz/7 tbsp butter or margarine
50g/2oz/¼ cup soft light brown sugar
60ml/4 tbsp chunky orange marmalade
1 egg, beaten
about 45ml/3 tbsp milk
60ml/4 tbsp glacé icing and shreds of orange and lemon rind, to decorate

1 Preheat the oven to 160°C/325°F/Gas 3. Lightly butter a 21 x 12cm/8½ x 4½in loaf tin (pan), then line the base with baking parchment and grease the paper.

2 Sift the flour, baking powder and cinnamon together, toss in the butter or margarine, then rub in using your fingertips or a pastry cutter until the mixture resembles coarse breadcrumbs. Stir in the sugar.

3 In a separate bowl, mix together the marmalade, egg and most of the milk, then stir into the flour mixture to make a soft dropping consistency, adding more milk if necessary.

4 Transfer the mixture to the tin and bake for 1¼ hours, or until firm to the touch. Leave the cake to cool in the tin for 5 minutes, then turn on to a wire rack, peel off the lining paper, and leave to cool completely.

5 Drizzle the glacé icing over the top of the cake and decorate with the orange and lemon rind.

Cook's Tip
To make citrus shreds, pare away strips of orange or lemon rind with a vegetable peeler, then cut into fine shreds with a knife.

Banana and Apricot Chelsea Buns

Old favourites get a new twist with a delectable fruity filling.

Serves 9

225g/8oz/2 cups strong white bread flour
10ml/2 tsp mixed (apple pie) spice
2.5ml/½ tsp salt
25g/1oz/2 tbsp soft margarine
7.5ml/1½ tsp easy-blend (rapid-rise) dried yeast
50g/2oz/¼ cup caster (superfine) sugar
90ml/6 tbsp hand-hot milk
1 egg, beaten

For the filling
1 large ripe banana
175g/6oz/1 cup ready-to-eat dried apricots
30ml/2 tbsp soft light brown sugar

For the glaze
30ml/2 tbsp caster (superfine) sugar
30ml/2 tbsp water

1 Grease an 18cm/7in square cake tin (pan). To prepare the filling, mash the banana in a bowl. Using kitchen scissors, cut up the apricots, and add to the bowl, then stir in the brown sugar. Mix together well.

2 Sift the flour, spice and salt into a large bowl. Rub in the margarine, then stir in the yeast and sugar. Make a well in the centre and pour in the milk and the egg. Mix to a soft dough, adding a little extra milk if necessary.

3 Turn the dough on to a floured surface and knead for 5 minutes until smooth and elastic. Roll out to a 30 x 23cm/ 12 x 9in rectangle. Spread the filling over the dough and roll up lengthways like a Swiss roll (jelly roll), with the join underneath. Cut into 9 pieces and place cut side downwards in the prepared tin. Cover and leave in a warm place until doubled in size, about 1½ hours.

4 Preheat the oven to 200°C/400°F/Gas 6. Bake the buns for 20–25 minutes, or until golden brown. Meanwhile make the glaze: mix the caster sugar and water in a small pan. Heat, stirring, until dissolved, then boil the mixture for 2 minutes. Brush the glaze over the buns while still hot, then remove from the tin and cool on a wire rack.

Teabread Energy 1725kcal/7238kJ; Protein 49.7g; Carbohydrate 209.3g, of which sugars 55.8g; Fat 82.5g, of which saturates 48.8g; Cholesterol 382mg; Calcium 408mg; Fibre 6.2g; Sodium 3324mg.
Chelsea Buns Energy 193kcal/817kJ; Protein 4.3g; Carbohydrate 38.4g, of which sugars 19.1g; Fat 3.5g, of which saturates 0.3g; Cholesterol 22mg; Calcium 70mg; Fibre 2.1g; Sodium 148mg.

Crunchy Muesli Muffins

These muesli muffins are great for breakfast.

Makes 10
150g/5oz/1¼ cups plain (all-purpose) flour, sifted
12.5ml/2½ tsp baking powder
30ml/2 tbsp caster (superfine) sugar
200g/7oz/1½ cups toasted oat cereal with raisins
250ml/8fl oz/1 cup milk
50g/2oz/¼ cup butter, melted, or corn oil
1 egg, beaten

1 Preheat the oven to 200°C/400°F/Gas 6. Grease 10 muffin cups or use paper cases.

2 Mix the flour, baking powder and sugar together in a large bowl. Stir in the oat cereal. In a separate bowl, combine the milk, melted butter or corn oil and the beaten egg. Add to the dry ingredients. Stir until moistened, but do not overmix.

3 Spoon the mixture into the cups, leaving room for the muffins to rise. Bake for 20 minutes, then transfer to a wire rack.

Cheese Muffins

Makes 9
50g/2oz/¼ cup butter, melted
175g/6oz/1½ cups plain (all-purpose) flour
10ml/2 tsp baking powder
30ml/2 tbsp caster (superfine) sugar
a pinch of salt
5ml/1 tsp paprika
2 eggs
120ml/4fl oz/½ cup milk
5ml/1 tsp dried thyme
50g/2oz mature (sharp) Cheddar cheese, cut into 1cm/½in dice

1 Preheat the oven to 190°C/375°F/Gas 5. Grease nine muffin cups or use paper cases. Sift the dry ingredients into a bowl.

2 Whisk the eggs, milk, butter and thyme in another bowl. Add to the dry ingredients and gently stir. Place a spoonful of batter into each cup. Add a few pieces of cheese to each and top with another spoonful of batter. Bake for 25 minutes, or until golden.

Raspberry Muffins

Adapt the traditional Cornish cream-tea tradition by serving these fabulous muffins barely warm, split and with a dollop of clotted cream.

Makes 12
50g/2oz/¼ cup butter, melted
115g/4oz/1 cup self-raising (self-rising) flour
115g/4oz/1 cup self-raising wholemeal (whole-wheat) flour
2.5ml/½ tsp salt
45ml/3 tbsp caster (superfine) sugar
2 eggs, beaten
200ml/7fl oz/scant 1 cup milk
175g/6oz/1 cup raspberries, fresh or frozen (defrosted for less than 30 minutes)

1 Melt the butter in a small pan over a low heat and then set it aside until required.

2 Preheat the oven to 190°C/375°F/Gas 5. Lightly grease 12 muffin cups, or use paper cases.

3 Sift the white and wholemeal flours with salt then tip in any wheat flakes left in the sieve. Add the caster sugar.

4 Beat the eggs, milk and melted butter together and stir into the dry ingredients to make a thick batter.

5 Stir the raspberries in gently. If you mix too much the raspberries begin to disintegrate and colour the dough. Spoon into the cups or paper cases.

6 Bake for 30 minutes, or until well risen and just firm to the touch. Leave to cool in the tin placed on a wire rack. Serve warm or cool.

> **Cook's Tips**
> *Frozen fruits, especially delicate ones like raspberries, are more likely to "bleed" into the batter than fresh soft fruits so just a quick stir will do. Frozen berries will also make the batter solidify so you need to add them and stir immediately.*

Crunchy Muesli Energy 199kcal/841kJ; Protein 5.4g; Carbohydrate 30.6g, of which sugars 4.6g; Fat 7g, of which saturates 3.1g; Cholesterol 31mg; Calcium 67mg; Fibre 1.8g; Sodium 55mg.
Cheese Muffins Energy 166kcal/698kJ; Protein 5.1g; Carbohydrate 19.3g, of which sugars 4.4g; Fat 8.1g, of which saturates 4.6g; Cholesterol 60mg; Calcium 93mg; Fibre 0.6g; Sodium 96mg.
Raspberry Muffins Energy 132kcal/555kJ; Protein 4g; Carbohydrate 19g, of which sugars 5.7g; Fat 5g, of which saturates 2.7g; Cholesterol 42mg; Calcium 48mg; Fibre 1.5g; Sodium 45mg.

Yogurt and Honey Muffins

Here is just the recipe for a relaxed Sunday breakfast: fragrant honey muffins served warm – heaven!

Makes 12

50g/2oz/4 tbsp butter
75ml/5 tbsp clear honey
250ml/8fl oz/1 cup natural (plain) yogurt
1 large (US extra large) egg, at room temperature
grated rind of 1 lemon
50ml/2fl oz/¼ cup lemon juice
150g/5oz/1¼ cups plain (all-purpose) flour
175g/6oz/1½ cups wholemeal (whole-wheat) flour
7.5ml/1½ tsp bicarbonate of soda (baking soda)
1.5ml/¼ tsp freshly grated nutmeg

1 Preheat the oven to 190°C/375°F/Gas 5. Grease 12 muffin cups or use paper cases.

2 In a pan, melt the butter and honey. Remove from the heat and set aside to cool slightly.

3 In a bowl, whisk together the yogurt, egg, lemon rind and juice. Add the butter and honey mixture. Set aside.

4 In another bowl, sift together the plain and wholemeal flours with the bicarbonate of soda and nutmeg. Fold them into the yogurt mixture to blend.

5 Fill the prepared cups two-thirds full. Bake until the tops spring back when touched lightly, about 20–25 minutes.

6 Cool in the tin (pan) for 5 minutes before turning out. Serve warm or at room temperature.

> **Variation**
> You can make these fabulous muffins more substantial by adding 50g/2oz/½ cup chopped walnuts with the flour at step 4, if you like.

Prune Muffins

Prunes bring a delightful moisture to these tasty and wholesome muffins.

Makes 12

1 egg
250ml/8fl oz/1 cup milk
120ml/4fl oz/½ cup vegetable oil
45g/1¾oz/scant ¼ cup caster (superfine) sugar
25g/1oz/2 tbsp soft dark brown sugar
275g/10oz/2½ cups plain (all-purpose) flour
10ml/2 tsp baking powder
2.5ml/½ tsp salt
1.5ml/¼ tsp freshly grated nutmeg
115g/4oz/½ cup cooked pitted prunes, chopped

1 Preheat the oven to 200°C/400°F/Gas 6. Grease 12 muffin cups or use paper cases.

2 Break the egg into a mixing bowl and beat with a fork. Beat in the milk and oil. Stir in the sugars and set aside.

3 Sift the flour, baking powder, salt and nutmeg into a mixing bowl. Make a well in the centre, pour in the egg mixture and stir until moistened. Do not overmix; the batter should be slightly lumpy. Finally, fold in the prunes.

4 Fill the prepared cups two-thirds full. Bake until golden brown, about 20 minutes. Leave to stand for 10 minutes before turning out. Serve warm or at room temperature.

> **Cook's Tip**
> Soak the prunes for a few hours before cooking in water to cover. They will take about 20 minutes to cook. Remove the pits from the cooked fruit.

> **Variation**
> Try this recipe with dried peaches, soaked and cooked as for the prunes. You could use orange juice instead of water, if you like.

Yogurt and Honey Energy 155kcal/652kJ; Protein 4.7g; Carbohydrate 25.4g, of which sugars 6.9g; Fat 4.6g, of which saturates 2.5g; Cholesterol 25mg; Calcium 66mg; Fibre 1.7g; Sodium 50mg.
Prune Energy 190kcal/801kJ; Protein 3.7g; Carbohydrate 28.1g, of which sugars 10.7g; Fat 7.8g, of which saturates 1.2g; Cholesterol 17mg; Calcium 66mg; Fibre 1.3g; Sodium 17mg.

Raspberry Buttermilk Muffins

The use of buttermilk and sunflower oil rather than butter makes these muffins particularly low in saturated fat.

Makes 10 – 12

275g/10oz/2¹/₂ cups plain
  (all-purpose) flour
15ml/1 tbsp baking powder
115g/4oz/¹/₂ cup caster
  (superfine) sugar
1 egg
250ml/8fl oz/1 cup buttermilk
60ml/4 tbsp sunflower oil
150g/5oz/scant 1 cup
  fresh raspberries

1 Preheat the oven to 200°C/400°F/Gas 6. Arrange 12 paper cases in a deep muffin tin (pan). Sift the flour and baking powder into a mixing bowl, stir in the sugar, then make a well in the centre.

2 Mix the egg, buttermilk and oil together in a jug (pitcher), pour into the bowl and mix quickly until just combined.

3 Add the raspberries and lightly fold in with a metal spoon. Spoon into the paper cases to within a third of the top.

4 Bake the muffins for 20–25 minutes, or until golden brown and firm in the middle. Remove to a wire rack and serve while it is still warm.

Variation
Use blackberries, blueberries or blackcurrants instead of raspberries if you prefer.

Cook's Tips
• To keep muffins as low fat as possible, paper cases are used for this recipe rather than greasing a muffin pan.
• This is a fairly moist batter which should only be lightly mixed. Over-mixing toughens the muffins and breaks up the fruit.

Date and Apple Muffins

These healthy muffins are delicious with morning coffee or breakfast. You will only need one or two per person as they are very filling.

Makes 12

150g/5oz/1¹/₄ cups self-raising
  (self-rising) wholemeal
  (whole-wheat) flour
150g/5oz/1¹/₄ cups self-raising
  (self-rising) white flour
5ml/1 tsp ground cinnamon
5ml/1 tsp baking powder
25g/1oz/2 tbsp soft margarine
75g/3oz/ 6 tbsp soft light
  brown sugar
250ml/8fl oz/1 cup apple juice
30ml/2 tbsp pear and
  apple spread
1 egg, lightly beaten
1 eating apple
75g/3oz/¹/₂ cup chopped dates
15ml/1 tbsp chopped
  pecan nuts

1 Preheat the oven to 200°C/400°F/Gas 6. Arrange 12 paper cases in a deep muffin tin (pan).

2 Put the wholemeal flour in a mixing bowl. Sift in the white flour with the cinnamon and baking powder.

3 Rub in the margarine until the mixture resembles breadcrumbs, then stir in the brown sugar.

4 In a bowl, stir a little of the apple juice with the pear and apple spread until smooth.

5 Add the remaining juice, mix well, then add to the rubbed-in mixture with the egg.

6 Peel and core the apple, chop the flesh finely and add it to the bowl with the dates. Mix quickly until just combined.

7 Divide the mixture between the muffin cases. Sprinkle with the chopped pecan nuts.

8 Bake the muffins for 20–25 minutes, or until golden brown and firm in the middle. Turn on to a wire rack and cool a little. Serve while still warm.

Raspberry Energy 165kcal/696kJ; Protein 3.6g; Carbohydrate 29.3g, of which sugars 11.9g; Fat 4.5g, of which saturates 0.7g; Cholesterol 17mg; Calcium 68mg; Fibre 1g; Sodium 17mg.
Date and Apple Energy 158kcal/670kJ; Protein 3.2g; Carbohydrate 30.7g, of which sugars 11.7g; Fat 3.4g, of which saturates 0.3g; Cholesterol 16mg; Calcium 45mg; Fibre 1g; Sodium 25mg.

Low-Fat Drop Scones

These little scones are quick and easy to make and contain very little fat.

Makes 18

225g/8oz/2 cups self-raising (self-rising) flour
2.5ml/½ tsp salt
15ml/1 tbsp caster (superfine) sugar
1 egg, beaten
300ml/½ pint/1¼ cups skimmed milk
oil, for brushing

1 Preheat a griddle, heavy frying pan or electric frying pan. Sift the flour and salt into a mixing bowl. Stir in the sugar and make a well in the centre.

2 Add the egg and half the milk. Stir from the centre to the outside, gradually incorporating the surrounding flour to make a smooth batter. Beat in the remaining milk.

3 Lightly grease the griddle or pan. Drop tablespoons of the batter on to the surface, making sure they are spaced well apart. Leave them to cook until they bubble and the bubbles begin to burst.

4 Turn the drop scones with a metal spatula and cook until the undersides are golden brown.

5 Keep the cooked drop scones warm and moist by wrapping them in a clean napkin while cooking successive batches. Serve with jam.

> **Variations**
> • *For Banana and Raisin Drop Scones mash two ripe bananas and add to the egg and half the milk before adding to the dry ingredients at step 2. Add 25g/1oz/¼ cup of raisins to the banana mixture and then stir in from the centre as before.*
> • *For a savoury version of these tasty scones, add 2 chopped spring onions (scallions) and 15ml/1 tbsp freshly grated Parmesan cheese to the batter. Serve with cottage cheese.*

Pineapple and Spice Drop Scones

Making the batter with pineapple or orange juice instead of milk cuts down on fat and adds to the taste. Semi-dried pineapple has an intense flavour that makes it ideal to use in baking.

Makes 24

115g/4oz/1 cup self-raising (self-rising) wholemeal (whole-wheat) flour
115g/4oz/1 cup self-raising (self-rising) white flour
5ml/1 tsp ground cinnamon
15ml/1 tbsp caster (superfine) sugar
1 egg, beaten
300ml/½ pint/1¼ cups pineapple juice
75g/3oz/½ cup semi-dried pineapple, chopped
oil, for brushing

1 Preheat a griddle, heavy frying pan or electric frying pan. Put the wholemeal flour in a mixing bowl. Sift in the white flour, ground cinnamon and sugar, and make a well in the centre of the dry ingredients.

2 Add the egg with half the pineapple juice. Stir from the centre to the outside, gradually incorporating the surrounding flour to make a smooth batter. Beat in the remaining juice with the chopped pineapple.

3 Lightly grease the griddle or pan. Drop tablespoons of the batter on to the surface, making sure they are spaced well apart. Leave them to cook until they bubble and the bubbles begin to burst.

4 Turn the drop scones with a metal spatula and cook until the underside is golden brown. Keep the cooked scones warm and moist by wrapping them in a clean napkin while cooking successive batches.

> **Cook's Tip**
> *Drop scones do not keep well – they are best eaten freshly cooked and taste especially good hot from the pan. These taste good with cottage cheese.*

Drop Scones Energy 55kcal/235kJ; Protein 2.1g; Carbohydrate 11.3g, of which sugars 1.8g; Fat 0.5g, of which saturates 0.1g; Cholesterol 11mg; Calcium 40mg; Fibre 0.4g; Sodium 12mg.
Pineapple and Spice Energy 45kcal/193kJ; Protein 1.2g; Carbohydrate 9.9g, of which sugars 2.6g; Fat 0.4g, of which saturates 0.1g; Cholesterol 8mg; Calcium 17mg; Fibre 0.4g; Sodium 3mg.

Buttermilk Scones

If time is short, drop heaped tablespoonfuls of the mixture on to the baking sheet.

Makes 10
225g/8oz/2 cups plain (all-purpose) flour

5ml/1 tsp baking powder
2.5ml/½ tsp bicarbonate of soda (baking soda)
5ml/1 tsp salt
50g/2oz/¼ cup butter or margarine, chilled
175ml/6fl oz/¾ cup buttermilk

1 Preheat the oven to 220°C/425°F/Gas 7. Sift the dry ingredients into a mixing bowl. Rub in the butter or margarine until the mixture resembles coarse breadcrumbs.

2 Add the buttermilk and combine well to form a soft dough. Turn on to a lightly floured surface and knead for 30 seconds.

3 Roll out to a 1cm/½in thickness. Cut rounds with a floured 6cm/2½in pastry (cookie) cutter. Transfer to a baking sheet and bake for 10–12 minutes. Serve with butter and honey.

Lavender Scones

Makes 12
225g/8oz/2 cups plain (all-purpose) flour
15ml/1 tbsp baking powder
50g/2oz/¼ cup butter

40g/1½oz/3 tbsp caster (superfine) sugar
10ml/2 tsp fresh lavender florets, chopped
about 175ml/6fl oz/¾ cup milk

1 Preheat the oven to 220°C/425°F/Gas 7. Grease a baking sheet. Sift the flour and baking powder into a bowl. Rub in the butter until the mixture resembles breadcrumbs.

2 Stir in the sugar and most of the lavender, reserving a little to decorate. Add enough milk to make a soft dough. Turn on to a floured surface and roll out to 2.5cm/1in thick. Cut 12 rounds with a floured cutter and place on the baking sheet. Brush the tops with milk and sprinkle with lavender. Bake for 10–12 minutes.

Date Scones

The rich taste of dates gives these scones a full flavour but you can adapt the recipe for use with ready-to-eat dried apricots or peaches as well.

Makes 12
225g/8oz/2 cups self-raising (self-rising) flour

a pinch of salt
50g/2oz/4 tbsp butter
50g/2oz/¼ cup caster (superfine) sugar
50g/2oz/⅓ cup finely chopped dates
150ml/¼ pint/⅔ cup milk
1 beaten egg, to glaze

1 Preheat the oven to 230°C/450°F/Gas 8. Sift the flour and salt into a bowl and rub in the butter using your fingertips or a pastry cutter until the mixture resembles fine breadcrumbs.

2 Add the sugar and chopped dates to the mixture, and stir to blend.

3 Make a well in the centre of the dry ingredients and add the milk. Stir with a fork until the mixture comes together into a fairly soft dough.

4 Turn the dough out on to a lightly floured surface and knead gently for 30 seconds. Roll it out to a 2cm/¾in thickness.

5 Cut out circles with a pastry (cookie) cutter. Arrange them, not touching, on an ungreased baking sheet, then glaze with the beaten egg.

6 Bake in the oven for 8–10 minutes, or until well risen and golden brown. Using a metal spatula, transfer the scones to a wire rack to cool completely.

> **Cook's Tip**
> For light and airy scones don't handle the dough too much and be careful not the roll it out too thinly or the scones will not rise sufficiently.

Buttermilk Scones Energy 120kcal/503kJ; Protein 2.7g; Carbohydrate 18.3g, of which sugars 1.1g; Fat 4.5g, of which saturates 2.7g; Cholesterol 11mg; Calcium 54mg; Fibre 0.7g; Sodium 235mg.
Lavender Scones Energy 115kcal/484kJ; Protein 2.3g; Carbohydrate 18.8g, of which sugars 4.5g; Fat 3.9g, of which saturates 2.4g; Cholesterol 10mg; Calcium 46mg; Fibre 0.6g; Sodium 32mg.
Date Scones Energy 128kcal/542kJ; Protein 2.4g; Carbohydrate 22.4g, of which sugars 8.1g; Fat 3.9g, of which saturates 2.4g; Cholesterol 10mg; Calcium 46mg; Fibre 0.8g; Sodium 32mg.

Sunflower Sultana Scones

Sunflower seeds give these fruit scones an interesting flavour and texture.

Makes 10–12

225g/8oz/2 cups self-raising (self-rising) flour
5ml/1 tsp baking powder
25g/1oz/2 tbsp soft sunflower margarine
30ml/2 tbsp golden caster (superfine) sugar
50g/2oz/⅓ cup sultanas (golden raisins)
30ml/2 tbsp sunflower seeds
150g/5oz/scant ⅔ cup natural (plain) yogurt
about 30–45ml/ 2–3 tbsp skimmed milk

1 Preheat the oven to 230°C/450°F/Gas 8. Lightly oil a baking sheet. Sift the flour and baking powder into a bowl and rub in the margarine evenly.

2 Stir in the sugar, sultanas and half the sunflower seeds, then mix in the yogurt, with just enough milk to make a fairly soft, but not sticky, dough.

3 Roll out on a lightly floured surface to about a 2cm/¾in thickness. Cut into 6cm/2½in flower shapes or rounds with a pastry (cookie) cutter and lift on to the baking sheet.

4 Brush with milk and sprinkle with the reserved sunflower seeds, then bake for 10–12 minutes, or until well risen and golden brown. Cool the scones on a wire rack. Serve split, spread with jam or low-fat spread.

Cook's Tip

Sunflower seeds are a wonder food, and a good and tasty way to add nutrients to the diet, especially selenium, which is often lacking. Don't buy too many at one time and source them from a store where they have a quick turnover so that the ones you buy are fresh. As sunflower seeds have a high fat content they don't store well for long periods. Buy small quantities at a time and put them in a sealed container in a cool place – even a refrigerator.

Cheese and Chive Scones

Feta cheese is used instead of butter in these delicious savoury scones, which make a tasty alternative to traditional scones.

Makes 9

115g/4oz/1 cup self-raising (self-rising) flour
150g/5oz/1 cup self-raising (self-rising) wholemeal (whole-wheat) flour
2.5ml/½ tsp salt
75g/3oz feta cheese
15ml/1 tbsp chopped fresh chives
150ml/¼ pint/⅔ cup milk, plus extra to glaze
1.5ml/¼ tsp cayenne pepper

1 Preheat the oven to 200°C/400°F/Gas 6. Sift the flours and salt into a large mixing bowl. Add any bran left in the sieve.

2 Crumble the feta cheese and rub it into the dry ingredients until the mixture resembles breadcrumbs. Stir in the chives, then add the milk and mix to a soft dough.

3 Turn the dough out on to a floured surface and lightly knead until smooth. Roll out to a 2cm/¾in thickness and stamp out scones with a 6cm/2½in pastry (cookie) cutter.

4 Transfer the scones to a non-stick baking sheet. Brush with milk, then sprinkle with the cayenne pepper. Bake for 15 minutes, or until risen and golden. Cool slightly on a wire rack before serving.

Variation

For Cheddar cheese and mustard scones, add 2.5ml/½ tsp mustard powder to the flours. Dice 50g/2oz/½ cup cold butter, and rub it into the dry ingredients until the mixture resembles breadcrumbs. Stir 50g/2oz/½ cup grated mature (sharp) Cheddar cheese into the mixture, then pour in the milk. Stir gently to make a soft dough. Roll out on a lightly floured surface and cut into triangles. Place on a baking sheet, brush with milk and sprinkle with 25g/1oz/¼ cup cheese. Bake for 15 minutes, or until well risen.

Cheese and Chive Energy 124kcal/524kJ; Protein 5.2g; Carbohydrate 21.5g, of which sugars 1.5g; Fat 2.5g, of which saturates 1.4g; Cholesterol 7mg; Calcium 74mg; Fibre 1.9g; Sodium 128mg.
Sunflower Sultana Energy 121kcal/513kJ; Protein 3g; Carbohydrate 21.2g, of which sugars 6.9g; Fat 3.3g, of which saturates 0.6g; Cholesterol 0mg; Calcium 99mg; Fibre 0.8g; Sodium 97mg.

Chive and Potato Scones

These little cakes should
be fairly thin, soft and crisp.
They are delicious served
warm with cottage cheese
as a filling yet low-fat snack
at any time of the day.

Makes 20
450g/1lb potatoes
115g/4oz/1 cup plain
  (all-purpose) flour, sifted
30ml/2 tbsp olive oil
30ml/2 tbsp chopped chives
salt and ground black pepper
low-fat spread, for topping

1 Cook the potatoes in a pan of boiling salted water for
20 minutes, then drain thoroughly. Return the potatoes to the
clean pan and mash them.

2 Preheat a griddle or heavy frying pan over low heat. Tip the
hot mashed potatoes into a bowl. Add the flour, olive oil and
chopped chives, with a little salt and ground black pepper. Mix
to a soft dough.

3 Roll out the dough on a well-floured surface to a thickness of
5mm/¼in. Stamp out rounds with a 5cm/2in scone (cookie)
cutter, re-rolling and cutting the trimmings, or cut into squares
with a sharp floured knife.

4 Cook the scones, in batches, on the hot griddle or frying pan
for about 10 minutes, or until they are golden brown. Keep the
heat low and turn the scones once.

5 Remove from the griddle or pan, top with a little low-fat
spread and serve immediately.

Cook's Tips
• Use floury potatoes such as King Edwards.
• The potatoes must be freshly cooked and mashed and should
not be allowed to cool before mixing.
• Cook the scones over low heat so that the outside does not
burn before the inside is cooked.

Ham and Tomato Scones

These make an ideal
accompaniment for soup.
If you have any left over the
next day, halve them, toast
under the grill (broiler) and
top with low-fat spread.

Makes 12
225g/8oz/2 cups self-raising
  (self-rising) flour
5ml/1 tsp mustard powder
5ml/1 tsp paprika, plus extra
  for topping

2.5ml/½ tsp salt
25g/1oz/2 tbsp soft margarine
50g/2oz Black Forest
  ham, chopped
15ml/1 tbsp chopped
  fresh basil
50g/2oz/½ cup drained
  sun-dried tomatoes in
  oil, chopped
90–120ml/3–4fl oz/⅓–½ cup
  skimmed milk, plus extra
  for brushing

1 Preheat the oven to 200°C/400°F/Gas 6. Flour a large
baking sheet.

2 Sift the flour, mustard, paprika and salt into a bowl. Rub in
the margarine, using your fingertips or a pastry cutter until the
mixture resembles breadcrumbs.

3 Stir in the ham, basil and sun-dried tomatoes; mix lightly.
Pour in enough milk to mix to a soft dough.

4 Turn the dough on to a lightly floured surface, knead lightly
and roll out to a 20 × 15cm/8 × 6in rectangle.

5 Cut into 5cm/2in squares and arrange on the baking sheet.

6 Brush sparingly with milk, sprinkle with paprika and bake for
12–15 minutes. Transfer to a wire rack to cool.

Cook's Tip
*Scone dough should be soft and moist and mixed for just long
enough to bind the ingredients together. Too much kneading
makes the scones tough.*

Cheese and Marjoram Scones

A great success for a hearty tea. With savoury toppings, these scones can make a good basis for a light lunch.

Makes 18

115g/4oz/1 cup plain (all-purpose) wholemeal (whole-wheat) flour
115g/4oz/1 cup self-raising (self-rising) flour
a pinch of salt
40g/1½oz/3 tbsp butter
1.5ml/¼ tsp dry mustard
10ml/2 tsp dried marjoram
50–75g/2–3oz/½–¾ cup finely grated Cheddar cheese
120ml/4fl oz/½ cup milk, or as required
50g/2oz/½ cup chopped pecan nuts or walnuts

1 Gently sift the two flours into a bowl and add the salt. Cut the butter into small pieces, and rub into the flour using your fingertips or a pastry cutter until the mixture resembles fine breadcrumbs.

2 Add the mustard, marjoram and grated cheese, and mix in sufficient milk to make a soft dough. Knead the dough lightly.

3 Preheat the oven to 220°C/425°F/Gas 7. Lightly grease two or three baking sheets.

4 Roll out the dough on a floured surface to about a 2cm/¾in thickness and cut it into 5cm/2in squares. Place the scones, slightly apart, on the baking sheets.

5 Brush the scones with a little milk and then sprinkle the chopped pecan nuts or walnuts over the top. Bake for about 12 minutes. Serve warm, spread with butter.

Cook's Tip
English mustard has been a traditional ingredient in many cheese dishes, as it sharpens the flavour of the cheese making it more pronounced. Always use dry mustard for adding to recipes such as the scones here or to pep up cheese toasts made with grated cheese, and remember: a little goes a long way.

Dill and Potato Cakes

Adding dill to these potato cakes makes them irresistible.

Makes 10

225g/8oz/2 cups self-raising (self-rising) flour
40g/1½oz/3 tbsp butter, softened
a pinch of salt
15ml/1 tbsp chopped fresh dill
175g/6oz/2 cups mashed potato, freshly made
30–45ml/2–3 tbsp milk

1 Preheat the oven to 230°C/450°F/Gas 8. Grease a baking sheet. Sift the flour into a bowl and add the butter, salt and dill. Mix in the mashed potato and enough milk to make a soft, pliable dough.

2 Roll out the dough on a well-floured surface until fairly thin. Cut into circles with a 7.5cm/3in pastry (cookie) cutter. Place the potato cakes on the baking sheet and bake them for 20–25 minutes, or until risen and golden.

Savoury Cheese Whirls

Makes 20

250g/9oz frozen puff pastry, thawed
15ml/1 tbsp vegetable extract
1 egg, beaten
50g/2oz/½ cup grated Cheddar cheese

1 Preheat the oven to 220°C/425°F/Gas 7. Grease a large baking sheet. Roll out the pastry on a lightly floured surface to a large rectangle, measuring about 35 x 25cm/14 x 10in.

2 Spread the pastry with vegetable extract, leaving a 1cm/½in border. Brush the edges of the pastry with egg and sprinkle over the cheese. Roll the pastry up quite tightly, starting from a long edge. Brush the outside of the pastry with beaten egg. Cut the pastry roll into slices 4cm/1½in thick and place on the baking sheet. Bake for 12–15 minutes, until the pastry is well risen and golden. Arrange on a serving plate and serve warm or cold with carrot and cucumber sticks.

Cheese and Marjoram Energy 121kcal/504kJ; Protein 3g; Carbohydrate 9.8g, of which sugars 0.9g; Fat 8g, of which saturates 2.4g; Cholesterol 8mg; Calcium 44mg; Fibre 1.1g; Sodium 39mg.
Potato Cakes Energy 121kcal/508kJ; Protein 2.6g; Carbohydrate 20.6g, of which sugars 0.6g; Fat 3.7g, of which saturates 2.2g; Cholesterol 9mg; Calcium 37mg; Fibre 0.9g; Sodium 27mg.
Cheese Whirls Energy 62kcal/259kJ; Protein 2g; Carbohydrate 4.6g, of which sugars 0.2g; Fat 4.2g, of which saturates 0.6g; Cholesterol 12mg; Calcium 28mg; Fibre 0g; Sodium 94mg.

Herb Popovers

Popovers are especially delicious when they are flavoured with herbs, and served as a snack.

Makes 12
3 eggs
250ml/8fl oz/1 cup milk

25g/1oz/2 tbsp butter, melted
75g/3oz/²⁄₃ cup plain
  (all-purpose) flour
1.5ml/¼ tsp salt
1 small sprig each mixed fresh
  herbs, such as chives,
  tarragon, dill and parsley

1 Preheat the oven to 220°C/425°F/Gas 7. Grease 12 small ramekins or individual baking cups.

2 With an electric mixer, beat the eggs until blended. Beat in the milk and melted butter.

3 Sift together the flour and salt, then beat into the egg mixture to combine thoroughly.

4 Strip the herb leaves from the stems and chop finely. Mix together and measure out 30ml/2 tbsp. Stir the measured herbs into the batter.

5 Half-fill the prepared ramekins or baking cups. Bake until golden, 25–30 minutes. Do not open the oven door during baking time or the popovers may collapse.

6 For drier popovers, pierce each one with a knife after 30 minutes' baking time and then bake for a further 5 minutes. Serve the herb popovers piping hot.

Variation
For basic plain popovers simply omit the herbs. To make a traditional popover heat a knob (pat) of dripping or lard (white cooking fat) in each cup of a patty tin (muffin pan). Heat the tin in the preheated oven and then pour in the batter until the cups are two-thirds full. Bake at the top of the oven as before.

Cheese Popovers

Serve these popovers simply as an accompaniment to a meal, or make a filling and serve them as an appetizer.

Makes 12
3 eggs
250ml/8fl oz/1 cup milk

25g/1oz/2 tbsp butter, melted
75g/3oz/²⁄₃ cup plain
  (all-purpose) flour
1.5ml/¼ tsp salt
1.5ml/¼ tsp paprika
25g/1oz/⅓ cup freshly grated
  Parmesan cheese

1 Preheat the oven to 220°C/425°F/Gas 7. Grease 12 small ramekins or individual baking cups.

2 With an electric mixer, beat the eggs until blended. Beat in the milk and melted butter.

3 Sift together the flour, salt and paprika, then beat into the egg mixture. Add the Parmesan cheese and stir in.

4 Half-fill the prepared cups and bake until golden, about 25–30 minutes. Do not open the oven door or the popovers may collapse.

5 For drier popovers, pierce each one with a knife after about 30 minutes' baking time and then bake for another 5 minutes. Serve hot.

Cook's Tips
• *Although some believe that batters for pancakes and popovers will be improved by resting for a while before cooking, this is not absolutely necessary. However, if you wish to prepare the batter in advance it can be left to stand for up to 4 hours, or 24 hours in a refrigerator.*
• *Always cook popovers on the top shelf of the oven.*
• *This recipe can be cooked in a well-greased, small baking tin (pan), if you prefer. It will take 35–40 minutes. Cut into wedges and serve warm.*

Herb Popovers Energy 65kcal/272kJ; Protein 2.9g; Carbohydrate 5.9g, of which sugars 1.1g; Fat 3.5g, of which saturates 1.7g; Cholesterol 53mg; Calcium 41mg; Fibre 0.2g; Sodium 39mg.
Cheese Popovers Energy 74kcal/311kJ; Protein 3.7g; Carbohydrate 5.9g, of which sugars 1.1g; Fat 4.2g, of which saturates 2.1g; Cholesterol 55mg; Calcium 66mg; Fibre 0.2g; Sodium 62mg.

Curry Crackers

These spicy, crisp little crackers are much lower in fat than other snacks.

Makes 12
50g/2oz/¹/₂ cup plain
 (all-purpose) flour
5ml/1 tsp curry powder
1.5ml/¹/₄ tsp chilli powder
1.5ml/¹/₄ tsp salt
15ml/1 tbsp chopped
 fresh coriander (cilantro)
30ml/2 tbsp water

1 Preheat the oven to 180°C/350°F/Gas 4. Sift the flour, curry powder, chilli powder and salt into a large bowl and make a well in the centre. Add the chopped coriander and water.

2 Stir from the centre outwards, gradually incorporating the flour and mixing to a fine dough.

3 Turn on to a lightly floured surface, and knead until smooth, then leave to rest for 5 minutes.

4 Cut the dough into 12 pieces and knead into small balls. Roll each ball out very thinly to a 10cm/4in round.

5 Arrange the rounds on two ungreased baking sheets. Bake for 15 minutes, turning over once during cooking.

Variations
These can be flavoured in many different ways. Omit the curry and chilli powders and add 15ml/1 tbsp caraway, fennel or mustard seeds. Any of the stronger spices such as nutmeg, cloves or ginger will give a good flavour but you will only need to add 5ml/1 tsp.

Cook's Tip
As this dough does not include yeast it only needs to be lightly kneaded; heavy handling is only suitable for yeast breads.

Oatcakes

Oatmeal not only tastes delicious, but it is also a good source of water-soluble fibre, is low in fat, and is thought to lower cholesterol levels. Try these delicious oatcakes spread with honey for a great start to the day.

Makes 8
175g/6oz/1¹/₂ cups medium
 oatmeal, plus extra
 for sprinkling
a pinch of bicarbonate of soda
 (baking soda)
2.5ml/¹/₂ tsp salt
15g/¹/₂oz/1 tbsp butter
75ml/5 tbsp water

1 Preheat the oven to 150°C/300°F/Gas 2. Grease a baking sheet. Put the oatmeal, bicarbonate of soda and salt in a large bowl and mix well.

2 Melt the butter with the water in a small pan. Bring to the boil, then add to the oatmeal and mix to a moist dough.

3 Turn the dough on to a surface sprinkled with oatmeal and knead to a smooth ball. Turn a large baking sheet upside down, sprinkle it lightly with oatmeal and place the ball of dough on top. Dust the top of the ball with oatmeal, then roll out thinly to a 25cm/10in round.

4 Stamp out rounds with a 5cm/2in scone (cookie) cutter, or cut the round into eight sections, ease apart slightly and bake for 50–60 minutes, or until crisp. Leave to cool on the baking sheet, then remove the oatcakes with a metal spatula.

Cook's Tips
• To get a neat circle, place a 25cm/10in cake board or plate on top of the oatcake. Cut away any excess dough with a palette knife, then remove the board or plate.
• Oatmeal is ground from the whole kernel of the cereal and is graded according to how finely it is ground, with the coarsest type known as pinhead. Medium oatmeal is widely available but fine is also suitable for oatcakes.

Curry Crackers Energy 14kcal/60kJ; Protein 0.4g; Carbohydrate 3.2g, of which sugars 0.1g; Fat 0.1g, of which saturates 0g; Cholesterol 0mg; Calcium 6mg; Fibre 0.1g; Sodium 49mg.
Oatcakes Energy 102kcal/429kJ; Protein 2.7g; Carbohydrate 15.9g, of which sugars 0g; Fat 3.5g, of which saturates 1g; Cholesterol 4mg; Calcium 12mg; Fibre 1.5g; Sodium 141mg.

Lemon Meringue Pie

Crisp on top and soft beneath, here is a classic dish whose popularity never seems to wane.

Serves 8
225g/8oz shortcrust pastry, thawed if frozen
grated rind and juice of 1 large lemon
250ml/8fl oz/1 cup plus 15ml/ 1 tbsp cold water
115g/4oz/generous ½ cup caster (superfine) sugar plus 90ml/ 6 tbsp extra
25g/1oz/2 tbsp butter
45ml/3 tbsp cornflour (cornstarch)
3 eggs, separated
a pinch of salt
a pinch of cream of tartar

1 Line a 23cm/9in pie dish with the pastry, folding under a 1cm/½in overhang to give a firm edge. Crimp the edge and chill for 20 minutes.

2 Preheat the oven to 200°C/400°F/Gas 6. Prick the pastry case base, line with baking parchment and fill with baking beans. Bake for 12 minutes.

3 Remove the paper and beans and bake until golden, 6–8 minutes more.

4 In a pan, combine the lemon rind and juice with 250ml/8fl oz/ 1 cup of the water, 115g/4oz/generous ½ cup of the sugar, and the butter. Bring to the boil.

5 Meanwhile, dissolve the cornflour in the remaining water. Add the egg yolks. Beat into the lemon mixture, return to the boil and whisk until thick, about 5 minutes. Cover the surface with baking parchment and leave to cool.

6 For the meringue, beat the egg whites, using an electric hand whisk, with the salt and cream of tartar until stiffly peaking. Add the remaining sugar a spoonful at a time and beat until glossy.

7 Spoon the lemon mixture into the pastry case. Spoon the meringue on top, sealing it with the pastry rim. Bake until golden, 12–15 minutes.

Blueberry Pie

Serve this tangy blueberry pie with crème fraîche, double (heavy) cream or vanilla ice cream.

Serves 6–8
450g/1lb shortcrust pastry, thawed if frozen
500g/1¼lb/5 cups blueberries
165g/5½oz/generous ¾ cup caster (superfine) sugar
45ml/3 tbsp plain (all-purpose) flour
5ml/1 tsp grated orange rind
1.5ml/¼ tsp freshly grated nutmeg
30ml/2 tbsp orange juice
5ml/1 tsp lemon juice

1 Preheat the oven to 190°C/375°F/Gas 5. On a lightly floured surface, roll out half of the pastry and use it to line a 23cm/9in pie dish that is 5cm/2in deep.

2 Combine the blueberries, 150g/5oz/¾ cup of the sugar, the flour, orange rind and nutmeg. Toss the mixture gently to coat all the fruit.

3 Pour the blueberry mixture into the pastry case and spread evenly. Sprinkle over the citrus juices.

4 Roll out the remaining pastry and use to cover the pie. Cut out small decorative shapes from the top. Use to decorate the pastry, and finish the edge.

5 Brush the top with water and sprinkle with the remaining caster sugar. Bake for 45 minutes, or until the pastry is golden brown. Serve warm or at room temperature.

Cook's Tip
To twist the edge of a double-crust pie hold the edges of the pie between your thumb and index finger and twist the edges together at 1cm/½in intervals. Alternatively, make a scalloped pattern by holding the finger of one hand against the top edge of the pie and squeezing the pastry with the thumb and forefinger of your other hand on the outside edge of the pie.

Meringue Pie Energy 254kcal/1067kJ; Protein 4.1g; Carbohydrate 33.4g, of which sugars 15.3g; Fat 12.6g, of which saturates 4.7g; Cholesterol 82mg; Calcium 44mg; Fibre 0.5g; Sodium 162mg.
Blueberry Pie Energy 371kcal/1559kJ; Protein 4.4g; Carbohydrate 55.8g, of which sugars 25.7g; Fat 16g, of which saturates 4.9g; Cholesterol 8mg; Calcium 93mg; Fibre 3.2g; Sodium 228mg.

Rhubarb and Cherry Pie

The unusual partnership of rhubarb and cherries works well in this fruity pie. Serve it warm, with a scoop of clotted cream or vanilla ice cream.

Serves 8
450g/1lb rhubarb, cut into 2.5cm/1in pieces
450g/1lb canned pitted tart red or black cherries, drained
275g/10oz/scant 1½ cups caster (superfine) sugar
45ml/3 tbsp quick-cooking tapioca milk, for glazing

For the pastry
275g/10oz/2½ cups plain (all-purpose) flour
5ml/1 tsp salt
75g/3oz/6 tbsp cold butter, diced
50g/2oz/4 tbsp cold white cooking fat or lard, diced
50–120ml/2–4fl oz/¼–½ cup iced water

1 To make the pastry, sift the flour and salt into a bowl. Add the butter and fat and rub in until the mixture resembles coarse breadcrumbs.

2 Stir in enough water to bind. Form into two balls, wrap in clear film (plastic wrap) and chill for 20 minutes.

3 Preheat a baking sheet in the oven at 200°C/400°F/Gas 6. Roll out one pastry ball and use to line a 23cm/9in pie dish, leaving a 1cm/½in overhang.

4 Mix together the rhubarb pieces, black cherries, caster sugar and tapioca, and spoon into the pastry case.

5 Roll out the remaining pastry ball, cut out four leaf shapes using a leaf cutter or a sharp knife, and use to cover the pie, leaving a 2cm/¾in overhang. Fold this overhang under the pastry base and flute to create an attractive edge. Roll small balls from the scraps, mark veins in the leaves and use to decorate the pie.

6 Glaze the top and bake on the baking sheet until golden, 40–50 minutes. Serve with clotted cream.

Festive Apple Pie

Warming spices transform this pie into a special dish.

Serves 8
900g/2lb cooking apples
15g/½oz/2 tbsp plain (all-purpose) flour
115g/4oz/generous ½ cup caster (superfine) sugar
25ml/1½ tbsp fresh lemon juice
2.5ml/½ tsp ground cinnamon
2.5ml/½ tsp mixed (apple pie) spice
1.5ml/¼ tsp ground ginger
1.5ml/¼ tsp freshly grated nutmeg
1.5ml/¼ tsp salt
50g/2oz/¼ cup butter, diced

For the pastry
275g/10oz/2½ cups plain (all-purpose) flour
5ml/1 tsp salt
75g/3oz/6 tbsp cold butter, diced
50g/2oz/4 tbsp cold white cooking fat or lard, diced
50–120ml/2–4fl oz/¼–½ cup iced water

1 To make the pastry, sift the flour and salt into a bowl. Add the butter and fat, and rub it in until the mixture resembles coarse breadcrumbs.

2 Stir in just enough water to bind the pastry. Form into two balls, wrap in clear film (plastic wrap) and chill in the refrigerator for 20 minutes.

3 Roll out one ball on a lightly floured surface, and use it to line a 23cm/9in pie dish. Preheat a baking sheet in the oven at 220°C/425°F/Gas 7.

4 Peel, core and slice the apples. Toss with the flour, sugar, lemon juice, cinnamon, mixed spice, ginger and nutmeg, and the salt. Spoon into the pastry case and dot with butter.

5 Roll out the remaining pastry ball. Place on top of the pie and trim to leave a 2cm/¾in overhang. Fold this under the pastry base and press to seal. Crimp the edge neatly. Form the scraps into leaf shapes and balls. Arrange on the pie and cut steam vents.

6 Bake on the baking sheet for 10 minutes. Reduce the heat to 180°C/350°F/Gas 4 and bake for 40 minutes, or until golden.

Cherry Pie Energy 442kcal/1868kJ; Protein 4.3g; Carbohydrate 78.9g, of which sugars 47.4g; Fat 14.4g, of which saturates 7.5g; Cholesterol 26mg; Calcium 129mg; Fibre 2.2g; Sodium 312mg.
Apple Pie Energy 392kcal/1644kJ; Protein 3.9g; Carbohydrate 53.3g, of which sugars 25.7g; Fat 19.6g, of which saturates 10.7g; Cholesterol 39mg; Calcium 66mg; Fibre 2.9g; Sodium 836mg.

Open Apple Pie

An open pie like this looks attractive and uses less pastry than a double-crust pie. If using eating apples for this pie, make sure they are firm-fleshed rather than soft.

Serves 8
1.3–1.6kg/3–3½lb tart eating or cooking apples
45g/1¾oz/scant ¼ cup caster (superfine) sugar
10ml/2 tsp ground cinnamon
grated rind and juice of 1 lemon

25g/1oz/2 tbsp butter, diced
30–45ml/2–3 tbsp honey, to glaze

For the pastry
275g/10oz/2½ cups plain (all-purpose) flour
2.5ml/½ tsp salt
115g/4oz/½ cup cold butter, diced
60g/2¼oz/4½ tbsp white cooking fat or lard, diced
75–90ml/5–6 tbsp iced water

1 To make the pastry, sift the flour and salt into a bowl. Add the butter and fat and rub in using your fingertips or a pastry cutter until the mixture resembles coarse breadcrumbs.

2 Stir in just enough water to bind the dough. Gather the dough into a ball, wrap in clear film (plastic wrap) and chill for at least 20 minutes.

3 Preheat the oven to 200°C/400°F/Gas 6. Place a baking sheet in the oven.

4 Peel, core and slice the apples thinly. Combine with the sugar, cinnamon, lemon rind and juice.

5 Roll out the pastry to a 30cm/12in circle. Use to line a 23cm/9in pie dish, leaving an overhanging edge. Fill with the apples. Fold in the edges and crimp loosely. Dot the apples with diced butter.

6 Bake on the hot baking sheet until the pastry is golden and the apples are tender, about 45 minutes.

7 Melt the honey in a pan and brush over the apples to glaze. Serve warm or at room temperature.

Apple and Cranberry Lattice Pie

Cranberries and raisins add colour and flavour to this pie.

Serves 8
grated rind of 1 orange
45ml/3 tbsp orange juice
2 large cooking apples
175g/6oz/1⅓ cups cranberries
65g/2½oz/½ cup raisins
25g/1oz/¼ cup chopped walnuts
215g/7½oz/generous 1 cup caster (superfine) sugar
115g/4oz/½ cup soft dark brown sugar

15g/½oz/2 tbsp plain (all-purpose) flour

For the pastry
275g/10oz/2½ cups plain (all-purpose) flour
2.5ml/½ tsp salt
75g/3oz/6 tbsp cold butter, diced
75g/3oz/½ cup cold white cooking fat or lard, diced
50–120ml/2–4fl oz/¼–½ cup iced water

1 To make the pastry, sift the flour and salt, add the butter and fat and rub in well using your fingertips or a pastry cutter. Stir in enough water to bind the dough. Form into two equal balls, wrap in clear film (plastic wrap) and chill for at least 20 minutes.

2 Put the orange rind and juice into a bowl. Peel and core the apples and grate into the bowl. Stir in the cranberries, raisins, walnuts, all except 15ml/1 tbsp of the caster sugar, the brown sugar and flour. Place a baking sheet in the oven and preheat to 200°C/400°F/Gas 6.

3 Roll out one ball of dough to about 3mm/⅛in thick. Transfer to a 23cm/9in pie plate and trim. Spoon the cranberry and apple mixture into the shell.

4 Roll out the remaining dough to a circle about 28cm/11in in diameter. With a serrated pastry wheel, cut the dough into 10 strips, 2cm/¾in wide. Place five strips horizontally across the top of the tart at 2.5cm/1in intervals. Weave in five vertical strips and trim. Sprinkle the top with the reserved sugar.

5 Bake for 20 minutes, then reduce the heat to 180°C/350°F/Gas 4 and bake for about 15 minutes more.

Open Apple Pie Energy 418kcal/1755kJ; Protein 4g; Carbohydrate 53.7g, of which sugars 27.5g; Fat 22.5g, of which saturates 12.2g; Cholesterol 44mg; Calcium 62mg; Fibre 4.1g; Sodium 112mg.
Lattice Pie Energy 528kcal/2223kJ; Protein 4.6g; Carbohydrate 83.3g, of which sugars 54.7g; Fat 22g, of which saturates 10.1g; Cholesterol 33mg; Calcium 86mg; Fibre 2.2g; Sodium 75mg.

Peach Leaf Pie

Pastry leaves top this most attractive spiced summer pie.

Serves 8
1.2kg/2½lb ripe peaches
juice of 1 lemon
90g/3½oz/½ cup caster
   (superfine) sugar
45ml/3 tbsp cornflour (cornstarch)
1.5ml/¼ tsp freshly grated nutmeg
2.5ml/½ tsp ground cinnamon
1 egg beaten with 15ml/1 tbsp
   water, to glaze

25g/1oz/2 tbsp cold
   butter, diced

For the pastry
275g/10oz/2½ cups plain
   (all-purpose) flour
4ml/¾ tsp salt
115g/4oz/½ cup cold
   butter, diced
60g/2¼oz/4½ tbsp cold
   white cooking fat or
   lard, diced
75–90ml/5–6 tbsp iced water

1 To make the pastry, sift the flour and salt into a bowl. Rub in the butter and fat using your fingertips or a pastry cutter until the mixture resembles breadcrumbs. Stir in just enough water to bind the dough. Gather into two balls, one slightly larger than the other. Wrap and chill for at least 20 minutes. Place a baking sheet in the oven and preheat to 220°C/425°F/Gas 7.

2 Drop the peaches into boiling water for 20 seconds, then transfer to a bowl of cold water. When cool, peel off the skins. Slice the flesh and combine with the lemon juice, sugar, cornflour and spices. Set aside.

3 Roll out the larger dough ball to 3mm/⅛in thick. Use to line a 23cm/9in pie plate. Chill. Roll out the remaining dough to 5mm/¼in thick. Cut out leaves 7.5cm/3in long. Mark veins. With the scraps, roll a few balls.

4 Brush the pastry base with egg glaze. Add the peaches and dot with the butter. Starting from the outside edge, cover the peaches with a ring of leaves. Place a second, staggered ring above. Continue until covered. Place the balls in the centre.

5 Brush with glaze. Bake for 10 minutes. Lower the heat to 180°C/350°F/Gas 4 and bake for 35–40 minutes more.

Walnut and Pear Lattice Pie

For the lattice top, either weave strips of pastry or use a special pastry cutter to create a lattice effect.

Serves 6–8
450g/1lb shortcrust pastry,
   thawed if frozen
450g/1lb pears, peeled, cored
   and thinly sliced
50g/2oz/¼ cup caster
   (superfine) sugar

25g/1oz/¼ cup plain
   (all-purpose) flour
2.5ml/½ tsp grated lemon rind
25g/1oz/generous ¼ cup raisins
   or sultanas (golden raisins)
25g/1oz/4 tbsp chopped walnuts
2.5ml/½ tsp ground cinnamon
50g/2oz/½ cup icing
   (confectioners') sugar
15ml/1 tbsp lemon juice
about 10ml/2 tsp cold water

1 Preheat the oven to 190°C/375°F/Gas 5. Roll out half of the pastry and use it to line a 23cm/9in tin that is about 5cm/2in deep.

2 Combine the pears, caster sugar, flour and lemon rind. Toss to coat the fruit. Mix in the raisins, nuts and cinnamon. Put the filling into the pastry case and spread it evenly.

3 Roll out the remaining pastry and use to make a lattice top. Bake the pie for 55 minutes, or until the pastry is golden brown on top.

4 Combine the icing sugar, lemon juice and water in a bowl and stir until smooth. Remove the pie from the oven. Drizzle the glaze evenly over the top, on the pastry and filling. Leave the pie to cool in its tin on a wire rack.

Variation
Try this tasty pie with apples instead of pears or combine fresh peaches or apricots with almonds instead of using pears and walnuts. To skin the peaches or apricots, drop them into boiling water for 20 seconds and then remove them and plunge them into cold water. Peel away the skins.

Peach Leaf Pie Energy 424kcal/1778kJ; Protein 4.8g; Carbohydrate 54.2g, of which sugars 22.8g; Fat 22.4g, of which saturates 12.2g; Cholesterol 44mg; Calcium 68mg; Fibre 3.1g; Sodium 112mg.
Pear Lattice Pie Energy 366kcal/1536kJ; Protein 4.3g; Carbohydrate 49.7g, of which sugars 21.5g; Fat 18.1g, of which saturates 5.1g; Cholesterol 8mg; Calcium 70mg; Fibre 2.6g; Sodium 228mg.

Lattice Berry Pie

Choose any berries you like for this handsome pie.

Serves 8
450g/1lb/about 4 cups berries, such as bilberries, blueberries and blackcurrants
115g/4oz/generous ½ cup caster (superfine) sugar
45ml/3 tbsp cornflour (cornstarch)
30ml/2 tbsp fresh lemon juice
25g/1oz/2 tbsp butter, diced

For the pastry
275g/10oz/2½ cups plain (all-purpose) flour
4ml/¾ tsp salt
115g/4oz/½ cup cold butter, diced
40g/1½oz/3 tbsp cold white cooking fat (shortening) or lard, diced
75–90ml/5–6 tbsp iced water
1 egg, beaten with 15ml/1 tbsp water, for glazing

1 To make the pastry, sift the flour and salt into a bowl. Add the butter and fat and rub in with your fingertips or a pastry cutter until the mixture resembles coarse breadcrumbs. Stir in just enough water to bind. Form into two balls, wrap in clear film (plastic wrap) and chill for 20 minutes.

2 Roll out one ball and use to line a 23cm/9in pie dish, leaving a 1cm/½in overhang. Brush the base with egg.

3 Mix the berries with the caster sugar, cornflour and lemon juice, reserving a few berries for decoration. Spoon this filling into the pastry case and dot with the butter. Brush egg around the pastry rim.

4 Preheat the oven to 220°C/425°F/Gas 7. Roll out the remaining pastry on a baking sheet lined with baking parchment. With a serrated pastry wheel, make 24 thin strips. Use the scraps to cut out leaf shapes, and mark veins.

5 Weave the strips in a close lattice and transfer to the pie. Seal the edges and trim. Arrange the leaves around the rim. Brush with egg and bake for 10 minutes.

6 Reduce the heat to 180°C/350°F/Gas 4 and bake the pie for a further 40–45 minutes. Decorate with the reserved berries.

Plum Pie

When the new season's plums are in the shops, treat someone special with this lightly spiced plum pie.

Serves 8
900g/2lb red or purple plums
grated rind of 1 lemon
15ml/1 tbsp fresh lemon juice
115–175g/4–6oz/generous ½– scant 1 cup caster (superfine) sugar
45ml/3 tbsp quick-cooking tapioca
1.5ml/¼ tsp salt
2.5ml/½ tsp ground cinnamon
1.5ml/¼ tsp freshly grated nutmeg

For the pastry
275g/10oz/2½ cups plain (all-purpose) flour
5ml/1 tsp salt
75g/3oz/6 tbsp cold butter, diced
50g/2oz/4 tbsp cold white cooking fat (shortening) or lard, diced
50–120ml/2–4fl oz/¼–½ cup iced water
milk, for glazing

1 To make the pastry, sift the flour and salt into a bowl. Add the butter and fat and rub in with your fingertips or a pastry cutter until the mixture resembles coarse breadcrumbs.

2 Stir in just enough water to bind the pastry. Form into two balls, wrap in clear film (plastic wrap) and chill for 20 minutes.

3 Preheat a baking sheet in the oven at 220°C/425°F/Gas 7. Roll out a pastry ball and use to line a 23cm/9in pie dish.

4 Halve and stone (pit) the plums, and chop roughly. Mix the lemon rind and juice, the chopped plums, caster sugar, tapioca and salt together in a bowl and mix in the spices, then transfer to the pastry-lined pie dish.

5 Roll out the remaining pastry, place on a baking sheet lined with baking parchment, and stamp out four hearts. Transfer the pastry lid to the pie using the paper.

6 Trim the pastry to leave a 2cm/¾in overhang. Fold this under the pastry base and pinch to seal. Arrange the hearts on top. Brush with milk and bake for 15 minutes. Reduce the heat to 180°C/350°F/Gas 4 and bake for a further 30–35 minutes.

Lattice Berry Pie Energy 384kcal/1607kJ; Protein 3.9g; Carbohydrate 50.4g, of which sugars 19g; Fat 19.9g, of which saturates 11.2g; Cholesterol 42mg; Calcium 69mg; Fibre 1.7g; Sodium 114mg.
Plum Pie Energy 360kcal/1516kJ; Protein 4.1g; Carbohydrate 57g, of which sugars 25.5g; Fat 14.5g, of which saturates 7.5g; Cholesterol 26mg; Calcium 73mg; Fibre 2.9g; Sodium 61mg.

Treacle Tart

Although called Treacle Tart, this old favourite is always made with syrup. It is straightforward to make – even this version with a simple lattice topping.

Serves 4–6
175ml/6fl oz/³/₄ cup golden (light corn) syrup
75g/3oz/1¹/₂ cups fresh white breadcrumbs
grated rind of 1 lemon
30ml/2 tbsp fresh lemon juice

For the pastry
175g/6oz/1¹/₂ cups plain (all-purpose) flour
2.5ml/¹/₂ tsp salt
75g/3oz/6 tbsp cold butter, diced
40g/1¹/₂oz/3 tbsp cold margarine, diced
45–60ml/3–4 tbsp iced water

1 To make the pastry, sift together the flour and salt, add the fats and rub in until the mixture resembles coarse breadcrumbs. Stir in enough water to bind.

2 Form into a ball, wrap in clear film (plastic wrap) and chill for 20 minutes.

3 Roll out the pastry and use to line a 20cm/8in pie dish. Chill for 20 minutes. Reserve the pastry trimmings.

4 Preheat a baking sheet in the oven at 200°C/400°F/Gas 6.

5 In a pan, warm the golden syrup until thin and runny. Stir in the breadcrumbs and lemon rind. Leave for 10 minutes, then stir in the lemon juice. Spread into the pastry case.

6 Roll out the pastry trimmings and cut into 12 thin strips. Lay six strips on the filling, then lay the other six at an angle over them to form a simple lattice.

7 Bake on the baking sheet for 10 minutes. Lower the heat to 190°C/375°F/Gas 5. Bake until golden, about 15 minutes more. Serve warm or cold.

Almond Syrup Tart

Almonds and a rich pastry make a treacle tart with a difference.

Serves 6
75g/3oz/1¹/₂ cups fresh white breadcrumbs
225g/8oz/scant 1 cup golden (light corn) syrup
finely grated rind of ¹/₂ lemon
10ml/2 tsp lemon juice
225g/8oz rich shortcrust pastry
25g/1oz/¹/₄ cup flaked (sliced) almonds
milk, to glaze (optional)
cream, custard or ice cream, to serve

1 Preheat the oven to 200°C/400°F/Gas 6. Line a 23cm/9in flan tin (pan) with the rich shortcrust pastry. Line the pastry with baking parchment and fill with baking beans.

2 Bake for 15 minutes and then remove the beans and paper and cook for 10 minutes more.

3 Combine the breadcrumbs with the golden syrup and the lemon rind and juice.

4 Spoon into the pastry case and spread out evenly. Sprinkle the flaked almonds evenly over the top.

5 Brush the pastry with milk to glaze, if you like. Bake for 25–30 minutes, or until the pastry and filling are golden brown.

6 Transfer to a wire rack to cool. Serve warm or cold, with cream, custard or ice cream.

Rich Shortcrust Pastry
Sift 150g/5oz/1¹/₄ cups plain (all-purpose) flour with a pinch of salt into a bowl. Add 75g/3oz/6 tbsp unsalted (sweet) butter or margarine cut into pieces, and rub in with your fingertips or a pastry cutter. Stir in 1 egg yolk, 7.5ml/1¹/₂ tsp caster (superfine) sugar and 15ml/1 tbsp water. Gather the dough together, wrap in clear film (plastic wrap) and chill for 30 minutes.

Treacle Tart Energy 373kcal/1567kJ; Protein 4.4g; Carbohydrate 55.5g, of which sugars 24g; Fat 16.3g, of which saturates 7.7g; Cholesterol 27mg; Calcium 64mg; Fibre 1.2g; Sodium 304mg.
Almond Syrup Tart Energy 407kcal/1712kJ; Protein 5.3g; Carbohydrate 63g, of which sugars 30.6g; Fat 16.6g, of which saturates 4.6g; Cholesterol 7mg; Calcium 75mg; Fibre 1.5g; Sodium 397mg.

Chocolate Pear Tart

Chocolate and pears have a natural affinity, well used in this luxurious pudding that makes an attractive dinner-party dessert.

Serves 8

115g/4oz plain (semisweet)
   chocolate, grated
3 large firm, ripe pears
1 egg
1 egg yolk
120ml/4fl oz/½ cup single
   (light) cream
2.5ml/½ tsp vanilla extract
45ml/3 tbsp caster
   (superfine) sugar

For the pastry

150g/5oz/1¼ cups plain
   (all-purpose) flour
1.5ml/¼ tsp salt
30ml/2 tbsp caster
   (superfine) sugar
115g/4oz/½ cup cold unsalted
   (sweet) butter, diced
1 egg yolk
15ml/1 tbsp lemon juice

1 To make the pastry, sift the flour and salt into a bowl. Add the sugar and butter. Rub in using your fingertips or a pastry cutter until the mixture resembles coarse breadcrumbs.

2 Stir in the egg yolk and lemon juice. Form a ball, wrap in clear film (plastic wrap), and chill for 20 minutes.

3 Preheat the oven to 200°C/400°F/Gas 6. Roll out the pastry and use to line a 25cm/10in flan (tart) dish.

4 Sprinkle the pastry case with the grated chocolate.

5 Peel, halve and core the pears. Cut in thin slices crossways, then fan out slightly. Transfer the pears to the tart using a metal spatula and arrange like spokes of a wheel.

6 Whisk together the egg and egg yolk, cream and vanilla extract. Ladle over the pears and sprinkle with sugar.

7 Bake on a baking sheet for 10 minutes. Reduce the heat to 180°C/350°F/Gas 4 and cook until the custard is set and the pears begin to caramelize, about 20 minutes more. Serve while still warm.

Pear and Apple Crumble Pie

This pie combines the old favourites of fruit pies and crumbles in one delicious treat. You could use just one fruit in this pie if you prefer.

Serves 8

3 firm pears
4 cooking apples
175g/6oz/scant 1 cup caster
   (superfine) sugar
30ml/2 tbsp cornflour (cornstarch)
1.5ml/¼ tsp salt
grated rind of 1 lemon
30ml/2 tbsp fresh lemon juice
75g/3oz/generous ½ cup raisins
75g/3oz/⅔ cup plain
   (all-purpose) flour
5ml/1 tsp ground cinnamon
75g/3oz/6 tbsp cold
   butter, diced

For the pastry

150g/5oz/1¼ cups plain
   (all-purpose) flour
2.5ml/½ tsp salt
65g/2½oz/5 tbsp cold white
   vegetable fat
   (shortening), diced
30ml/2 tbsp iced water

1 To make the pastry, sift the flour and salt into a bowl. Add the fat and rub in using your fingertips until the mixture resembles breadcrumbs. Stir in enough water to bind.

2 Wrap in clear film (plastic wrap) and chill for 30 minutes. Form into a ball, roll out, and use to line a 23cm/9in pie dish, leaving a 1cm/½in overhang. Fold this under for double thickness. Flute the edge, then chill.

3 Preheat a baking sheet in the oven at 230°C/450°F/Gas 8. Peel, core and slice the fruit. Quickly combine in a bowl with one-third of the sugar, the cornflour, salt, lemon rind and juice, and the raisins.

4 For the crumble topping, combine the remaining sugar, flour, cinnamon and butter in a bowl. Rub in until the mixture resembles coarse breadcrumbs. Spoon the filling into the pastry case. Sprinkle the crumbs over the top.

5 Bake on the baking sheet for 10 minutes, then reduce the heat to 180°C/350°F/Gas 4. Cover the pie loosely with foil and bake for a further 35–40 minutes.

Pear Tart Energy 357kcal/1493kJ; Protein 4.8g; Carbohydrate 39.5g, of which sugars 25.1g; Fat 21.1g, of which saturates 12.4g; Cholesterol 114mg; Calcium 68mg; Fibre 2.2g; Sodium 106mg.
Crumble Pie Energy 390kcal/1639kJ; Protein 3.3g; Carbohydrate 61.3g, of which sugars 39.9g; Fat 16.3g, of which saturates 8.2g; Cholesterol 28mg; Calcium 65mg; Fibre 3.1g; Sodium 190mg.

Pear and Hazelnut Flan

A delicious flan for Sunday lunch. Grind the hazelnuts yourself if you prefer, or use ground almonds instead.

Serves 6–8
115g/4oz/1 cup plain
   (all-purpose) flour
115g/4oz/1 cup plain wholemeal
   (whole-wheat) flour
115g/4oz/¹⁄₂ cup sunflower
   margarine
45ml/3 tbsp cold water

For the filling
50g/2oz/¹⁄₂ cup self-raising
   (self-rising) flour
115g/4oz/1 cup ground hazelnuts
5ml/1 tsp vanilla extract
50g/2oz/¹⁄₄ cup caster
   (superfine) sugar
50g/2oz/¹⁄₄ cup butter, softened
2 eggs, beaten
400g/14oz can pears in
   natural juice
45ml/3 tbsp raspberry jam
few chopped hazelnuts, to decorate

1 For the pastry, stir the flours together, then rub in the margarine using your fingertips or a pastry cutter until the mixture resembles fine breadcrumbs. Mix to a firm dough with the water.

2 Roll out the dough and use to line a 23–25cm/9–10in flan tin (tart pan), pressing it up the sides after trimming, so that the pastry sits a little above the tin. Prick the base with a fork, line with baking parchment and fill with baking beans. Chill for 30 minutes.

3 Preheat the oven to 200°C/400°F/Gas 6. Place the flan tin on a baking sheet and bake blind for 20 minutes. Remove the paper and beans after 15 minutes.

4 To make the filling beat together the flour, hazelnuts, vanilla extract, sugar and eggs. If the misture is too thick, stir in some of the juice from the canned pears.

5 Reduce the oven temperature to 180°C/350°F/Gas 4. Spread the jam on the pastry case and spoon over the filling.

6 Drain the pears and arrange them, cut side down, in the filling. Sprinkle over the nuts for decoration. Bake for 30 minutes, or until risen, firm and golden brown.

Latticed Peaches

When fresh peaches are out of season, make this elegant dessert using canned peach halves instead.

Serves 6
115g/4oz/1 cup plain
   (all-purpose) flour
45ml/3 tbsp butter or
   sunflower margarine
45ml/3 tbsp natural (plain) yogurt
30ml/2 tbsp orange juice
milk, to glaze

For the filling
3 ripe peaches
45ml/3 tbsp ground almonds
30ml/2 tbsp natural
   (plain) yogurt
finely grated rind of
   1 small orange
1.5ml/¹⁄₄ tsp almond extract

For the sauce
1 ripe peach
45ml/3 tbsp orange juice

1 Lightly grease a baking sheet. Sift the flour into a bowl and rub in the butter or margarine. Stir in the yogurt and orange juice to make a firm dough. Roll out half the pastry thinly and stamp out six rounds with a 7.5cm/3in cookie cutter. Place on the baking sheet.

2 Drop the peaches into boiling water for 20 seconds. Remove and plunge into cold water. Remove the skins, halve and remove the stones (pits). Mix together the almonds, yogurt, orange rind and almond extract. Spoon into the hollows of each peach half and place, cut side down, on the pastry rounds.

3 Roll out the remaining pastry thinly and cut into thin strips. Arrange the strips over the peaches to form a lattice, brushing with milk to secure firmly. Trim the ends. Chill for 30 minutes.

4 Preheat the oven to 200°C/400°F/Gas 6. Brush with milk and bake for 15–18 minutes, or until golden brown.

5 To make the sauce, skin the peach as before and halve it to remove the stone. Place the flesh in a food processor or blender, with the orange juice, and purée until the mixture is smooth. Serve the peaches hot, with the peach sauce spooned around them.

Hazelnut Flan Energy 389kcal/1626kJ; Protein 7.6g; Carbohydrate 40.9g, of which sugars 16g; Fat 22.8g, of which saturates 3.5g; Cholesterol 49mg; Calcium 69mg; Fibre 3.6g; Sodium 138mg.
Latticed Peaches Energy 196kcal/822kJ; Protein 4.7g; Carbohydrate 21.6g, of which sugars 6.8g; Fat 10.8g, of which saturates 4.3g; Cholesterol 16mg; Calcium 75mg; Fibre 1.9g; Sodium 59mg.

Orange Tart

If you like oranges, this is the dessert for you!

Serves 8

200g/7oz/1 cup caster (superfine) sugar
250ml/8fl oz/1 cup fresh orange juice, strained
2 large navel oranges
165g/5½oz/scant 1 cup whole blanched almonds
50g/2oz/¼ cup butter
1 egg
15ml/1 tbsp plain (all-purpose) flour
45ml/3 tbsp apricot jam

For the pastry

210g/7½oz/scant 2 cups plain (all-purpose) flour
2.5ml/½ tsp salt
50g/2oz/¼ cup cold butter, diced
40g/1½oz/3 tbsp cold margarine, diced
45–60ml/3–4 tbsp iced water

1 To make the pastry, sift the flour and salt into a bowl. Add the butter and margarine, and rub in using your fingertips or a pastry cutter until the mixture resembles coarse breadcrumbs. Stir in just enough water to bind the dough. Wrap and chill for 20 minutes.

2 Roll out the pastry to a 5mm/¼ in thickness. Use to line a 20cm/8in flan tin (pan). Trim and chill until needed.

3 In a pan, combine 165g/5½oz/¾ cup of the sugar and the orange juice and boil until thick and syrupy. Cut the unpeeled oranges into 5mm/¼in slices. Add to the syrup. Simmer gently for 10 minutes. Put on a wire rack to dry. When cool, cut in half. Reserve the syrup. Place a baking sheet in the oven and heat to 200°C/400°F/Gas 6.

4 Grind the almonds finely in a blender or food processor. Cream the butter and remaining sugar until light and fluffy. Beat in the egg and 30ml/2 tbsp of the orange syrup. Stir in the almonds and flour.

5 Melt the jam over a low heat, then brush over the pastry case. Pour in the almond mixture. Bake on the baking sheet until set, about 20 minutes, then cool. Arrange overlapping orange slices on top. Boil the remaining syrup until thick and brush over the top to glaze.

Raspberry Tart

A luscious tart of rich custard beneath juicy fresh raspberries.

Serves 8

4 egg yolks
65g/2½oz/generous ¼ cup caster (superfine) sugar
45ml/3 tbsp plain (all-purpose) flour
300ml/½ pint/1¼ cups milk
1.5ml/¼ tsp salt
2.5ml/½ tsp vanilla extract
450g/1lb/2⅔ cups fresh raspberries
75ml/5 tbsp redcurrant jelly
15ml/1 tbsp orange juice

For the pastry

185g/6½oz/1⅔ cups plain (all-purpose) flour
2.5ml/½ tsp baking powder
1.5ml/¼ tsp salt
15ml/1 tbsp sugar
grated rind of ½ orange
75g/3oz/6 tbsp cold butter, diced
1 egg yolk
45–60ml/3–4 tbsp whipping cream

1 To make the pastry, sift the flour, baking powder and salt into a bowl. Stir in the sugar and orange rind. Add the butter and rub in using your fingertips or a pastry cutter until the mixture resembles breadcrumbs. Stir in the egg yolk and cream to bind. Form into a ball, wrap in clear film (plastic wrap) and chill.

2 For the filling, beat the egg yolks and sugar until thick and creamy. Gradually stir in the flour. Bring the milk and salt just to the boil, then remove from the heat. Whisk into the egg yolk mixture, return to the pan and continue whisking over a medium-high heat until just bubbling. Cook for 3 minutes to thicken. Transfer to a bowl. Stir in the vanilla extract, then cover with baking parchment.

3 Preheat the oven to 200°C/400°F/Gas 6. Roll out the pastry and use to line a 25cm/10in pie dish. Prick the base with a fork, line with baking parchment and fill with baking beans. Bake for 15 minutes. Remove the paper and beans, and bake until golden, about 6–8 minutes more. Leave to cool.

4 Spread an even layer of the custard filling in the pastry case and arrange the raspberries on top. Melt the redcurrant jelly and orange juice in a pan and brush over the top to glaze.

Orange Tart Energy 500kcal/2093kJ; Protein 8.6g; Carbohydrate 59.4g, of which sugars 37.4g; Fat 27g, of which saturates 7.7g; Cholesterol 50mg; Calcium 130mg; Fibre 3.1g; Sodium 137mg.
Raspberry Tart Energy 323kcal/1359kJ; Protein 6.9g; Carbohydrate 44g, of which sugars 22.1g; Fat 14.6g, of which saturates 7.8g; Cholesterol 154mg; Calcium 126mg; Fibre 2.3g; Sodium 86mg.

Chocolate Nut Tart

This is a sophisticated tart – strictly for grown-ups!

Serves 6 – 8
225g/8oz sweet shortcrust pastry, thawed if frozen
200g/7oz/1¾ cups dry amaretti
90g/3½oz/generous ½ cup blanched almonds
50g/2oz/⅓ cup blanched hazelnuts
45ml/3 tbsp caster (superfine) sugar
200g/7oz plain (semisweet) cooking chocolate
45ml/3 tbsp milk
50g/2oz/¼ cup butter
45ml/3 tbsp amaretto liqueur or brandy
30ml/2 tbsp single (light) cream

1 Grease a shallow loose-based 25cm/10in flan tin (pan). Roll out the pastry on a lightly floured surface, and use it to line the tin. Trim the edge, prick the base with a fork and chill for 30 minutes.

2 Grind the amaretti in a blender or food processor. Tip into a mixing bowl.

3 Set eight whole almonds aside and place the rest in the food processor or blender with the hazelnuts and sugar. Grind to a medium texture. Add the nuts to the amaretti, and mix well to combine thoroughly.

4 Preheat the oven to 190°C/375°F/Gas 5. Slowly melt the chocolate with the milk and butter in the top of a double boiler or in a heatproof bowl over a pan of simmering water. Once the chocolate has melted, stir until smooth.

5 Pour the chocolate mixture into the dry ingredients, and mix well. Add the liqueur or brandy and the cream.

6 Spread the filling evenly in the pastry case. Bake for 35 minutes, or until the crust is golden brown and the filling has puffed up and is beginning to darken.

7 Allow to cool to room temperature. Split the reserved almonds in half and use to decorate the tart.

Pecan Nut Tartlets

These delightful individual tartlets make an elegant dinner-party dessert.

Serves 6
425g/15oz shortcrust pastry, thawed if frozen
175g/6oz/1 cup pecan nut halves
3 eggs, beaten
25g/1oz/2 tbsp butter, melted
275g/10oz/¾ cup golden (light corn) syrup
2.5ml/½ tsp vanilla extract
115g/4oz/generous ½ cup caster (superfine) sugar
15ml/1 tbsp plain (all-purpose) flour

1 Preheat the oven to 180°C/350°F/Gas 4. Roll out the pastry and use to line six 10cm/4in tartlet tins (muffin pans). Divide the pecan nut halves between the pastry cases.

2 Combine the eggs with the butter, and add the golden syrup and vanilla extract. Sift over the caster sugar and flour, and blend well. Fill the pastry cases with the mixture and leave until the nuts rise to the surface.

3 Bake for 35–40 minutes, or until a skewer inserted into the centre comes out clean. Cool in the tins for 15 minutes, then turn out on to a wire rack to cool completely.

Basic Shortcrust Pastry
Mix together 225g/8oz/1 cups flour, a pinch of salt and 115g/4oz/½ cup butter. Using your fingertips or a pastry cutter, rub the butter into the flour until the mixture resembles fine breadcrumbs. Mix in the water and gather together to form a firm dough. Wrap the dough in clear film (plastic wrap) and chill for 30 minutes. Use this recipe when 350g/12oz pastry is required – enough to line a 23cm/9in flan tin (tart pan). For 425g/15oz pastry you will need 275g/10oz flour to 150g/5oz butter.
• If you use half butter and half white vegetable fat (shortening) you will have a lighter and less rich crust.
• For Sweet Shortcrust Pastry, add 50g/2oz/¼ cup sugar to the flour.

Nut Tart Energy 644kcal/2685kJ; Protein 9.6g; Carbohydrate 56.4g, of which sugars 32g; Fat 42.4g, of which saturates 13.4g; Cholesterol 21mg; Calcium 122mg; Fibre 3g; Sodium 241mg.
Tartlets Energy 828kcal/3463kJ; Protein 10.6g; Carbohydrate 95g, of which sugars 58.2g; Fat 47.8g, of which saturates 11.2g; Cholesterol 115mg; Calcium 118mg; Fibre 2.9g; Sodium 486mg.

Peach Roll

This is the perfect light cake for a summer afternoon tea in the garden.

Serves 6–8
3 eggs
115g/4oz/generous ½ cup caster (superfine) sugar
75g/3oz/⅔ cup plain (all-purpose) flour, sifted
15ml/1 tbsp boiling water
90ml/6 tbsp peach jam
icing (confectioners') sugar, for dusting (optional)

1 Preheat the oven to 200°C/400°F/Gas 6. Line and grease a 30 x 20cm/12 x 8in Swiss roll tin (jelly roll pan).

2 Combine the eggs and sugar in a bowl. Beat with a hand-held electric whisk until thick and mousse-like: when the whisk is lifted a trail should remain on the surface of the mixture for at least 30 seconds.

3 Carefully fold in the flour with a large metal spoon, then add the boiling water in the same way.

4 Spoon the mixture into the prepared tin, spread evenly to the edges and bake for 10–12 minutes, or until the cake springs back when lightly pressed.

5 Spread a sheet of baking parchment on a flat surface and sprinkle it with caster sugar. Carefully invert the cake on top and peel off the lining paper.

6 Make a neat cut two-thirds of the way through the cake, about 1cm/½in from the short edge nearest you – this will make it easier for you to roll the sponge cake. Trim the remaining edges to give a neat finish to the cake.

7 Spread the cake with the peach jam and roll up quickly from the partially cut end. Hold in position for a minute, making sure the join is underneath.

8 Cool on a wire rack. Dust with icing sugar, if you like.

Chestnut and Orange Roulade

A very moist roulade with a sweet and creamy filling – ideal to serve as an impressive low-fat dessert.

Serves 8
3 eggs, separated
115g/4oz/generous ½ cup caster (superfine) sugar
½ x 439g/15½ oz can unsweetened chestnut purée
grated rind and juice of 1 orange
icing (confectioners') sugar, for dusting

For the filling
225g/8oz/1 cup low-fat soft cheese
15ml/1 tbsp clear honey
1 orange

1 Preheat the oven to 180°C/350°F/Gas 4. Line and grease a 30 x 20cm/12 x 8in Swiss roll tin (jelly roll pan).

2 Whisk the egg yolks and sugar in a bowl until thick. Put the chestnut purée into a separate bowl. Whisk the orange rind and juice into the purée, then whisk into the egg mixture.

3 Whisk the egg whites until fairly stiff. Stir a spoonful into the chestnut mixture, then fold in the remaining egg whites.

4 Spoon the mixture into the prepared tin and bake for 30 minutes, or until firm. Cool for 5 minutes in the tin, then cover with a clean damp dish towel and leave until completely cold.

5 Meanwhile, make the filling. Put the soft cheese in a bowl with the honey. Finely grate the orange rind and add to the bowl. Using a sharp knife, cut away all the peel and pith from the orange. Cut the fruit into segments, cutting either side of the membrane so that you have only the flesh. Chop roughly and set aside. Add any juice to the bowl, then beat until smooth. Mix in the orange segments.

6 Sprinkle a sheet of baking parchment with icing sugar. Turn the roulade out on to the paper; peel off the lining paper. Spread the filling over the roulade and roll up like a Swiss roll (jelly roll). Transfer to a plate and dust with icing sugar.

Peach Roll Energy 146kcal/618kJ; Protein 3.4g; Carbohydrate 30.1g, of which sugars 22.9g; Fat 2.2g, of which saturates 0.6g; Cholesterol 71mg; Calcium 33mg; Fibre 0.3g; Sodium 31mg.
Roulade Energy 176kcal/741kJ; Protein 7.2g; Carbohydrate 28.1g, of which sugars 19.9g; Fat 5.1g, of which saturates 2.2g; Cholesterol 78mg; Calcium 64mg; Fibre 1.1g; Sodium 154mg.

Pound Cake with Red Fruit

This orange-scented cake is good for tea, or served as a dessert with cream.

Makes one 20 x 10cm/ 8 x 4in cake
450g/1lb/4 cups fresh raspberries, strawberries or pitted cherries, or a combination of any of these
175g/6oz/generous ¾ cup caster (superfine) sugar, plus 15–30ml/ 1–2 tbsp, plus extra for sprinkling
15ml/1 tbsp lemon juice
175g/6oz/1½ cups plain (all-purpose) flour
10ml/2 tsp baking powder
pinch of salt
175g/6oz/¾ cup unsalted (sweet) butter, softened
3 eggs
grated rind of 1 orange
15ml/1 tbsp orange juice

1 Reserve a few whole fruits for decorating. In a blender or food processor, process the fruit until smooth. Add 15–30ml/1–2 tbsp sugar and the lemon juice, and process again. Strain the sauce and chill.

2 Grease the base and sides of a 20 x 10cm/8 x 4in loaf tin (pan) and line the base with baking parchment. Grease the paper. Sprinkle with sugar and tip out any excess. Preheat the oven to 180°C/350°F/Gas 4.

3 Sift together the flour, baking powder and a pinch of salt. In another bowl, beat the butter until creamy. Add the sugar and beat until light and fluffy. Add the eggs, one at a time, beating well after each addition.

4 Beat in the orange rind and juice. Gently fold the flour mixture into the butter mixture in three batches, then spoon the mixture into the loaf tin and tap gently to release any air bubbles.

5 Bake for 35–40 minutes, or until the top is golden and it is springy to the touch. Leave the cake in its tin on a wire rack for 10 minutes, then remove the cake from the tin and cool for 30 minutes. Remove the paper and serve slices of cake with a little of the fruit sauce, decorated with the reserved fruit.

Madeleines

These little tea cakes, baked in a special tin with shell-shaped cups, are best eaten on the day they are made.

Makes 12
165g/5½oz/generous 1¼ cups plain (all-purpose) flour
5ml/1 tsp baking powder
2 eggs
75g/3oz/¾ cup icing (confectioners') sugar, plus extra for dusting
grated rind of 1 lemon or orange
15ml/1 tbsp lemon or orange juice
75g/3oz/6 tbsp unsalted (sweet) butter, melted and slightly cooled

1 Preheat the oven to 190°C/375°F/Gas 5. Generously grease a 12-cup madeleine tin (pan). Sift together the flour and the baking powder.

2 Beat the eggs and icing sugar in a large bowl until the mixture is thick and creamy and leaves ribbon trails. Gently fold in the lemon or orange rind and juice.

3 Beginning with the flour mixture, alternately fold in the flour and melted butter in four batches. Leave to stand for 10 minutes, then spoon into the tin. Tap gently to release any air bubbles.

4 Bake for 12–15 minutes, rotating the tin halfway through cooking. The cake is cooked when a skewer inserted in the centre comes out clean.

5 Turn out on to a wire rack to cool completely and dust with icing sugar before serving.

Cook's Tip
These cakes look sweet baked in the traditional Madeleine tins (pans), but cooking equipment suppliers now stock all kinds of novelty cake tins, such as flowers, stars and hearts that would be suitable for using with this recipe. You could even drizzle some orange-flavoured glacé icing over the tops.

Pound Cake Energy 2927kcal/12264kJ; Protein 43.5g; Carbohydrate 341.9g, of which sugars 208.6g; Fat 164.1g, of which saturates 96.6g; Cholesterol 944mg; Calcium 569mg; Fibre 16.7g; Sodium 1301mg.
Madeleines Energy 130kcal/547kJ; Protein 2.4g; Carbohydrate 17.3g, of which sugars 6.8g; Fat 6.2g, of which saturates 3.5g; Cholesterol 45mg; Calcium 28mg; Fibre 0.4g; Sodium 50mg.

Angel Cake

This heavenly cake contains virtually no fat and tastes simply divine! Serve in slices with fresh fruit for a delicious healthy dessert.

Makes one 25cm/10in cake

130g/4½oz/generous 1 cup
  sifted plain (all-purpose) flour
30ml/2 tbsp cornflour (cornstarch)
285g/10½oz/1½ cups caster
  (superfine) sugar
10 egg whites
6.5ml/1¼ tsp cream of tartar
1.5ml/¼ tsp salt
5ml/1 tsp vanilla extract
1.5ml/¼ tsp almond extract
icing (confectioners') sugar,
  for dusting

1 Preheat the oven to 160°C/325°F/Gas 3. Sift the flours before measuring, then sift them four times together with 90g/3½oz/ ½ cup of the sugar.

2 Beat the egg whites until foamy. Sift over the cream of tartar and salt and beat until the egg whites form soft peaks.

3 Add the remaining sugar in three batches, beating well after each addition.

4 Stir in the vanilla and almond extracts. Fold in the flour mixture in two batches.

5 Transfer to an ungreased 25cm/10in cake tin (pan) and bake until just browned on top, about 1 hour.

6 Turn the tin upside-down on to a wire rack and cool for 1 hour. Then invert on to a serving plate. Lay a star-shaped template on top of the cake, sift over some icing sugar and remove the template.

Cook's Tip
For an exceptionally light sponge cake such as this one it is important to sift the dry ingredients several times to help incorporate air into the batter. Be careful to fold in the flour to the wet ingredients so that the air will not be lost.

Iced Angel Cake

Served with fromage frais or low-fat yogurt and fresh raspberries, this makes a light dessert.

Serves 10

40g/1½oz/scant ½ cup
  cornflour (cornstarch)
40g/1½oz/scant ½ cup plain
  (all-purpose) flour
8 egg whites
225g/8oz/generous 1 cup caster
  (superfine) sugar, plus extra
  for sprinkling
5ml/1 tsp vanilla extract
icing (confectioners') sugar, for dusting

For the topping
175g/6oz/1½ cups icing
  (confectioners') sugar
15–30ml/1–2 tbsp lemon juice
physalis to decorate (optional)

1 Preheat the oven to 180°C/350°F/Gas 4. Sift both flours into a bowl.

2 Whisk the egg whites in a large grease-free bowl until very stiff, then gradually add the sugar and vanilla extract, a spoonful of sugar at a time, whisking until the mixture is thick and glossy.

3 Fold in the flour mixture with a large metal spoon. Spoon into an ungreased 25cm/10in angel cake tin, smooth the surface and bake for 40–45 minutes.

4 Sprinkle a piece of baking parchment with caster sugar and set an egg cup in the centre. Invert the cake tin over the paper, balancing the cake on the egg cup. When cold, the cake will drop out of the tin. Transfer it to a plate.

5 To make the lemon icing, mix the icing sugar with the lemon juice until you get a smooth paste. Pour on to the cake, and decorate with the physalis, if using.

Cook's Tip
You can also bake this cake in a 20cm/8in cake tin (pan); it will probably take a little longer to cook. When it is well-risen and springy to the touch it is done.

Angel Cake Energy 131kcal/558kJ; Protein 4.1g; Carbohydrate 30.3g, of which sugars 23.6g; Fat 0.1g, of which saturates 0g; Cholesterol 0mg; Calcium 20mg; Fibre 0.1g; Sodium 80mg.
Iced Angel Cake Energy 179kcal/762kJ; Protein 4.3g; Carbohydrate 43.4g, of which sugars 30g; Fat 0.2g, of which saturates 0g; Cholesterol 0mg; Calcium 35mg; Fibre 0.4g; Sodium 65mg.

Tangy Lemon Cake

The lemon syrup forms a crusty topping when it has completely cooled. Leave the cake in the tin until ready to serve.

Makes one 900g/2lb loaf

175g/6oz/³⁄4 cup butter
175g/6oz/scant 1 cup caster (superfine) sugar

3 eggs, beaten
175g/6oz/1¹⁄2 cups self-raising (self-rising) flour
grated rind of 1 orange
grated rind of 1 lemon

For the syrup

115g/4oz/generous ¹⁄2 cup caster (superfine) sugar
juice of 2 lemons

1 Preheat the oven to 180°C/350°F/Gas 4. Grease a 900g/2lb loaf tin (pan).

2 Beat the butter and sugar together until light and fluffy, then gradually beat in the eggs.

3 Fold in the flour and the orange and lemon rinds.

4 Turn the mixture into the prepared loaf tin and bake for 1¹⁄4–1¹⁄2 hours, or until set in the centre, risen and golden.

5 Remove the loaf from the oven, but leave it in the tin rather than turning out on to a wire rack.

6 To make the syrup, gently heat the sugar in a small pan with the lemon juice until the sugar has completely dissolved, then boil for 15 seconds.

7 Pour the syrup over the hot cake in the tin and leave to cool completely.

> **Cook's Tip**
> *You can use a skewer to pierce holes over the cake's surface so that the syrup will drizzle through and soak into the cake. There will still be a crusty, sugary top, but the cake itself will be moist.*

Pineapple and Apricot Cake

This is not a long-keeping cake, but it does freeze, well wrapped in baking parchment and then foil.

Makes one 18cm/7in square or 20cm/8in round cake

175g/6oz/³⁄4 cup unsalted (sweet) butter
150g/5oz/generous ³⁄4 cup caster (superfine) sugar
3 eggs, beaten

few drops vanilla extract
225g/8oz/2 cups plain all-purpose) flour
1.5ml/¹⁄4 tsp salt
7.5ml/1¹⁄2 tsp baking powder
225g/8oz/1 cup ready-to-eat dried apricots, chopped
115g/4oz/¹⁄2 cup each chopped crystallized ginger and crystallized pineapple
grated rind and juice of ¹⁄2 orange
grated rind and juice of ¹⁄2 lemon
a little milk

1 Preheat the oven to 180°C/350°F/Gas 4. Double line an 18cm/7in square or 20cm/8in round cake tin (pan).

2 Cream the butter and sugar together until light and fluffy.

3 Gradually beat in the eggs with the vanilla extract, beating well after each addition.

4 Sift together the flour, salt and baking powder. Add a little of the flour with the last of the egg, then fold in the remainder.

5 Gently fold in the apricots, ginger and pineapple and the orange and lemon rinds, then add sufficient fruit juice and milk to give the batter a fairly soft dropping consistency.

6 Spoon the batter into the prepared cake tin and smooth the top with a wet spoon.

7 Bake for 20 minutes, then reduce the oven temperature to 160°C/325°F/Gas 3 and bake for a further 1¹⁄2–2 hours, or until a skewer inserted into the centre comes out clean.

8 Leave the cake to cool completely in the tin. Wrap in fresh paper before storing in an airtight tin.

Tangy Lemon Energy 2849kcal/11927kJ; Protein 36.3g; Carbohydrate 331.9g, of which sugars 201.9g; Fat 162.6g, of which saturates 96.2g; Cholesterol 944mg; Calcium 830mg; Fibre 5.4g; Sodium 1912mg.
Apricot Cake Energy 3400kcal/14276kJ; Protein 52.3g; Carbohydrate 455.1g, of which sugars 283.7g; Fat 165.6g, of which saturates 96.3g; Cholesterol 944mg; Calcium 748mg; Fibre 25.9g; Sodium 1326mg.

Carrot Cake with Geranium Cheese

The scented cheese topping makes this carrot cake special.

Makes one 23 x 12cm/ 9 x 5in cake

115g/4oz/1 cup self-raising (self-rising) flour
5ml/1 tsp bicarbonate of soda (baking soda)
2.5ml/½ tsp ground cinnamon
2.5ml/½ tsp ground cloves
200g/7oz/scant 1 cup soft brown sugar
225g/8oz/generous 1½ cups grated carrot
150g/5oz/scant 1 cup sultanas (golden raisins)

150g/5oz/½ cup finely chopped preserved stem ginger
150g/5oz/scant 1 cup pecan nuts
150ml/¼ pint/⅔ cup sunflower oil
2 eggs, lightly beaten

For the topping
2 or 3 lemon-scented geranium leaves
225g/8oz/2 cups icing (confectioners') sugar
60g/2¼oz/generous 4 tbsp cream cheese
30g/1¼oz/generous 2 tbsp softened butter
5ml/1 tsp grated lemon rind

1 For the topping, put the geranium leaves, torn into small pieces, in a small bowl and mix with the icing sugar. Leave in a warm place overnight for the sugar to take up the scent.

2 For the cake, sift the flour, bicarbonate of soda and spices together. Add the sugar, grated carrots, sultanas, stem ginger and pecan nuts. Stir well, then add the oil and beaten eggs. Mix with an electric mixer for 5 minutes.

3 Preheat the oven to 180°C/350°F/Gas 4. Then grease a 23 x 13cm/9 x 5in loaf tin (pan), line the base with baking parchment, and grease the paper. Pour the mixture into the tin and bake for about 1 hour. Remove the cake from the oven, leave to stand for a few minutes, and then cool on a wire rack.

4 Meanwhile, make the cream cheese topping. Remove the pieces of geranium leaf from the icing sugar and discard. Place the cream cheese, butter and lemon rind in a bowl. Using an electric mixer, gradually add the icing sugar, beating well until smooth. Spread over the top of the cooled cake.

Peach and Amaretto Cake

Try this delicious cake for dessert, with reduced-fat fromage frais, or serve it solo for afternoon tea.

Serves 8

3 eggs, separated
175g/6oz/¾ cup caster (superfine) sugar
grated rind and juice of 1 lemon
50g/2oz/½ cup semolina
40g/1½oz/scant ½ cup ground almonds

25g/1oz/¼ cup plain (all-purpose) flour

For the syrup
75g/3oz/6 tbsp caster (superfine) sugar
90ml/6 tbsp water
30ml/2 tbsp amaretto liqueur
2 peaches or nectarines, halved and stoned (pitted)
60ml/4 tbsp apricot jam, sieved, to glaze

1 Preheat the oven to 180°C/350°F/Gas 4. Grease a 20cm/8in round loose-based cake tin (pan). Whisk the egg yolks, caster sugar, lemon rind and juice in a bowl until thick, pale and creamy, then fold in the semolina, almonds and flour until the mixture is smooth.

2 Whisk the egg whites in a grease-free bowl until fairly stiff. Using a metal spoon, stir a generous spoonful of the whites into the semolina mixture to lighten it, then fold in the remaining egg whites. Spoon into the prepared cake tin.

3 Bake for 30–35 minutes, then remove the cake from the oven and carefully loosen the edges. Prick the top with a skewer and leave to cool slightly in the tin.

4 Meanwhile, make the syrup. Heat the sugar and water in a small pan, stirring until dissolved, then boil without stirring for 2 minutes. Add the amaretto liqueur and drizzle slowly over the cake. Leave to cool in the tin.

5 Remove the cake from the tin and transfer it to a serving plate. Slice the peaches or nectarines and arrange them in concentric circles over the top of the cake. Brush the fruit with the glaze.

Carrot Cake Energy 5413kcal/22706kJ; Protein 47.4g; Carbohydrate 740.3g, of which sugars 649.3g; Fat 272.2g, of which saturates 57.6g; Cholesterol 502mg; Calcium 789mg; Fibre 21.4g; Sodium 624mg.
Amaretto Cake Energy 244kcal/1034kJ; Protein 4.7g; Carbohydrate 46.7g, of which sugars 39.4g; Fat 5g, of which saturates 0.8g; Cholesterol 71mg; Calcium 47mg; Fibre 0.9g; Sodium 32mg.

Cranberry and Apple Ring

Tangy cranberries add an unusual flavour to this moist cake, which is best eaten very fresh.

Makes one ring cake
225g/8oz/2 cups self-raising (self-rising) flour
5ml/1 tsp ground cinnamon
75g/3oz/scant ½ cup light muscovado (brown) sugar
1 eating apple, cored and diced
75g/3oz/¾ cup fresh or frozen cranberries
60ml/4 tbsp sunflower oil
150ml/¼ pint/⅔ cup apple juice
cranberry jelly and apple slices, to decorate

1 Preheat the oven to 180°C/350°F/Gas 4. Lightly grease a 1-litre/1¾-pint/4-cup ring tin (pan) with oil.

2 Sift together the flour and ground cinnamon in a large bowl, then stir in the light muscovado sugar.

3 Toss together the diced apple and cranberries in a small bowl.

4 Stir the apple mixture into the dry ingredients, then add the oil and apple juice and beat together until everything is thoroughly combined.

5 Spoon the cake mixture into the prepared ring tin and bake for 35–40 minutes, or until the cake is firm to the touch.

6 Leave the cake in the tin for 5 minutes, then turn out on to a wire rack and leave to cool completely.

7 To serve, arrange apple slices over the cake and drizzle warmed cranberry jelly over the top.

Cook's Tip
This moist, tangy ring would be an ideal alternative to Christmas cake for those who do not like such dense, rich cakes. It would also be a good way of using up any left-over cranberries or cranberry jelly.

Greek Honey and Lemon Cake

A wonderfully moist and tangy cake, you could ice it if you wished.

Makes one 19cm/7½in square cake
40g/1½oz/3 tbsp sunflower margarine
60ml/4 tbsp clear honey
finely grated rind and juice of 1 lemon
150ml/¼ pint/⅔ cup milk
150g/5oz/1¼ cups plain (all-purpose) flour
7.5ml/1½ tsp baking powder
2.5ml/½ tsp freshly grated nutmeg
50g/2oz/⅓ cup semolina
2 egg whites
10ml/2 tsp sesame seeds

1 Preheat the oven to 200°C/400°F/Gas 6. Lightly oil and base-line a 19cm/7½in square deep cake tin (pan).

2 Place the margarine and 45ml/3 tbsp of the honey in a pan and heat gently until melted.

3 Reserve 15ml/1 tbsp lemon juice, then stir in the rest with the lemon rind and milk.

4 Sift together the flour, baking powder and nutmeg, then beat in with the semolina. Whisk the egg whites until they form soft peaks, then fold evenly into the mixture.

5 Spoon into the cake tin and sprinkle with sesame seeds. Bake for 25–30 minutes, or until golden brown. Mix the reserved honey and lemon juice, and drizzle over the cake while warm. Cool in the tin, then cut into fingers to serve.

Cook's Tip
Baking powder is a useful raising agent for making cakes and is used with plain (all-purpose) flour. When mixed with a liquid it forms a gas that causes the cake to rise. It also acts further when the cake is baked. Always check the use-by date on the packet and replace as necessary for successful baking.

Apple Ring Energy 1565kcal/6610kJ; Protein 22.1g; Carbohydrate 280.7g, of which sugars 109.2g; Fat 47.2g, of which saturates 5.7g; Cholesterol 0mg; Calcium 371mg; Fibre 9.2g; Sodium 17mg.
Lemon Cake Energy 1307kcal/5510kJ; Protein 32.4g; Carbohydrate 208.7g, of which sugars 55.6g; Fat 43.8g, of which saturates 9.2g; Cholesterol 12mg; Calcium 474mg; Fibre 6.5g; Sodium 525mg.

Cherry Batter Cake

This colourful tray bake looks pretty cut into neat squares or fingers. Its unusual topping makes it especially tasty.

Makes one 33 x 23cm/ 13 x 9in cake
225g/8oz/2 cups self-raising (self-rising) flour
5ml/1 tsp baking powder
75g/3oz/6 tbsp butter, softened
150g/5oz/scant 1 cup soft light brown sugar
1 egg, lightly beaten

150ml/¼ pint/⅔ cup milk
icing (confectioners') sugar, for dusting
whipped cream, to serve (optional)

For the topping
675g/1½lb jar black cherries or blackcurrants, drained
175g/6oz/¾ cup soft light brown sugar
50g/2oz/½ cup self-raising (self-rising) flour
50g/2oz/¼ cup butter, melted

1 Preheat the oven to 190°C/375°F/Gas 5. Grease and line a 33 x 23cm/13 x 9in Swiss roll tin (jelly roll pan) with baking parchment, and grease the paper.

2 To make the base, sift the flour and baking powder into a large bowl. Add the butter, sugar, egg and milk.

3 Beat until the mixture becomes smooth, then turn into the prepared tin and smooth the surface.

4 To make the topping, sprinkle the drained cherries or blackcurrants evenly over the batter mixture.

5 Mix together the brown sugar, flour and melted butter, and spoon evenly over the fruit.

6 Bake for 40 minutes, or until the top is golden brown and the centre is firm to the touch.

7 Leave to cool for 15 minutes in the tin, then turn out and leave on a wire rack to cool completely. Dust with icing sugar. Serve with whipped cream, if you like.

Lemon and Apricot Cake

This cake is soaked in a tangy lemon syrup after baking to keep it really moist.

Makes one 23 x 13cm/ 9 x 5in loaf
175g/6oz/¾ cup butter, softened
175g/6oz/1½ cups self-raising (self-rising) flour
2.5ml/½ tsp baking powder
175g/6oz/generous ¾ cup caster (superfine) sugar
3 eggs, lightly beaten
finely grated rind of 1 lemon

175g/6oz/1½ cups ready-to-eat dried apricots, finely chopped
75g/3oz/¾ cup ground almonds
40g/1½oz/6 tbsp pistachio nuts, chopped
50g/2oz/½ cup flaked (sliced) almonds
15g/½oz/2 tbsp whole pistachio nuts

For the syrup
45ml/3 tbsp caster (superfine) sugar
freshly squeezed juice of 1 lemon

1 Preheat the oven to 180°C/350°F/Gas 4. Grease and line a 23 x 13cm/9 x 5in loaf tin (pan) with baking parchment and grease the paper.

2 Place the butter in a large bowl. Sift over the flour and baking powder, then add the sugar, eggs and lemon rind.

3 Using an electric whisk or a wooden spoon, beat for 1–2 minutes, or until smooth and glossy, then stir in the apricots, ground almonds and chopped pistachio nuts.

4 Spoon the mixture into the loaf tin and smooth the surface. Sprinkle with the flaked almonds and the whole pistachio nuts.

5 Bake for 1¼ hours, or until a skewer inserted into the centre of the cake comes out clean. Check the cake after 45 minutes and cover with a piece of foil when the top is nicely browned. Leave the cake to cool in the tin.

6 To make the lemon syrup, gently dissolve the sugar in the lemon juice in a small pan over a low heat. Spoon the syrup over the cake. When the cake is completely cooled, turn it carefully out of the tin and peel off the lining paper.

Apricot Cake Energy 4358kcal/18221kJ; Protein 80.6g; Carbohydrate 443.9g, of which sugars 305.8g; Fat 264g, of which saturates 105.8g; Cholesterol 944mg; Calcium 967mg; Fibre 29.1g; Sodium 1622mg.
Cherry Batter Energy 3770kcal/15932kJ; Protein 43g; Carbohydrate 686g, of which sugars 476.4g; Fat 114.4g, of which saturates 68.8g; Cholesterol 466mg; Calcium 890mg; Fibre 12.6g; Sodium 974mg.

Jewel Cake

This pretty cake is excellent served as a teatime treat.

Makes one 23 x 13cm/ 9 x 5in cake
115g/4oz/¹/₂ cup mixed glacé
   (candied) cherries, halved,
   washed and dried
50g/2oz/4 tbsp preserved stem
   ginger in syrup, chopped,
   washed and dried
50g/2oz/¹/₃ cup chopped mixed
   (candied) peel
115g/4oz/1 cup self-raising
   (self-rising) flour
75g/3oz/²/₃ cup plain
   (all-purpose) flour

25g/1oz/¹/₄ cup cornflour
   (cornstarch)
175g/6oz/³/₄ cup butter
175g/6oz/scant 1 cup caster
   (superfine) sugar
3 eggs
grated rind of 1 orange

To decorate
175g/6oz/1¹/₂ cups icing
   (confectioners') sugar, sifted
30–45ml/2–3 tbsp freshly
   squeezed orange juice
50g/2oz/¹/₄ cup mixed glacé
   (candied) cherries, chopped
25g/1oz/2¹/₂ tbsp mixed
   (candied) peel, chopped

1 Preheat the oven to 180°C/350°F/Gas 4. Grease and line a 23 x 13cm/9 x 5in loaf tin (pan) and grease the paper.

2 Place the glacé cherries, stem ginger and mixed peel in a plastic bag with 25g/1oz/¹/₄ cup of the self-raising flour and shake to coat evenly. Sift together the remaining flours and cornflour.

3 In a large bowl, beat together the butter and sugar until light and fluffy. Beat in the eggs, one at a time. Fold in the sifted flours with the orange rind, then stir in the dried fruit.

4 Transfer the mixture to the cake tin and bake for 1¼ hours, or until a skewer inserted into the centre comes out clean. Leave in the tin for 5 minutes, then cool on a wire rack.

5 For the decoration, mix the icing sugar with the orange juice until smooth. Drizzle the icing over the cake.

6 Mix together the glacé cherries and mixed peel, then use to decorate the cake. Allow the icing to set before serving.

Apple Cake

A deliciously moist cake with a silky icing.

Makes one ring cake
675g/1¹/₂lb apples, peeled, cored
   and quartered
500g/1¹/₄lb/generous 4¹/₂ cups
   caster (superfine) sugar
15ml/1 tbsp water
350g/12oz/3 cups plain
   (all-purpose) flour
9ml/1³/₄ tsp bicarbonate of soda
   (baking soda)
5ml/1 tsp ground cinnamon

5ml/1 tsp ground cloves
175g/6oz/generous 1 cup raisins
150g/5oz/1¹/₄ cups
   chopped walnuts
225g/8oz/1 cup butter or
   margarine, at room temperature
5ml/1 tsp vanilla extract

For the icing
115g/4oz/1 cup icing
   (confectioners') sugar
1.5ml/¹/₄ tsp vanilla extract
30–45ml/2–3 tbsp milk

1 Put the apples, 50g/2oz/¹/₄ cup of the sugar and the water in a pan and bring to the boil. Simmer for 25 minutes, stirring occasionally to break up any lumps. Leave to cool. Preheat the oven to 160°C/325°F/Gas 3. Thoroughly butter and flour a 1.75-litre/3-pint/7¹/₂-cup tube tin (pan).

2 Sift the flour, bicarbonate of soda and spices into a bowl. Remove 30ml/2 tbsp of the mixture to another bowl and toss with the raisins and 115g/4oz/1 cup of the walnuts.

3 Cream the butter or margarine and remaining sugar together until light and fluffy. Fold in the apple mixture gently. Fold the flour mixture into the apple mixture. Stir in the vanilla extract and the raisin and walnut mixture. Pour into the tube tin. Bake until a skewer inserted in the centre comes out clean, about 1¹/₂ hours. Cool completely in the tin on a wire rack, then unmould on to the rack.

4 To make the icing, put the sugar in a bowl and stir in the vanilla extract and 15ml/1 tbsp milk. Add more milk until the icing is smooth and has a thick pouring consistency. Transfer the cake to a serving plate and drizzle the icing over the top. Sprinkle with the remaining nuts. Allow the icing to set.

Jewel Cake Energy 4369kcal/18404kJ; Protein 41.5g; Carbohydrate 726.1g, of which sugars 560.5g; Fat 164.9g, of which saturates 96.5g; Cholesterol 982mg; Calcium 1042mg; Fibre 11.5g; Sodium 2007mg.
Apple Cake Energy 7049kcal/29657kJ; Protein 66.1g; Carbohydrate 1103.7g, of which sugars 835.9g; Fat 294.1g, of which saturates 126.6g; Cholesterol 482mg; Calcium 1141mg; Fibre 30.4g; Sodium 1553mg.

Dorset Apple Cake

Serve this fruity apple cake warm, and spread with butter if you like.

Makes one 18cm/7in round cake

225g/8oz cooking apples, peeled, cored and chopped
juice of ½ lemon
225g/8oz/2 cups plain (all-purpose) flour
7.5ml/1½ tsp baking powder
115g/4oz/½ cup butter, diced
165g/5½oz/¾ cup soft light brown sugar
1 egg, beaten
about 30–45ml/2–3 tbsp milk, to mix
2.5ml/½ tsp ground cinnamon

I Preheat the oven to 180°C/350°F/Gas 4. Grease and line an 18cm/7in round cake tin (pan).

2 Toss the apple with the lemon juice and set aside. Sift the flour and baking powder together, then rub in the butter using your fingertips or a pastry cutter, until the mixture resembles breadcrumbs.

3 Stir in 115g/4oz/1 cup of the brown sugar, the apple and the egg, and mix well, adding sufficient milk to make a soft dropping consistency.

4 Transfer the batter to the prepared tin. In a bowl, mix together the remaining sugar and the cinnamon. Sprinkle over the cake mixture, then bake for 45–50 minutes, or until golden. Leave to cool in the tin for 10 minutes, then transfer to a wire rack to cool completely.

Cook's Tips

For successful cakes remember these few golden rules:
• Heat the oven to the correct temperature in plenty of time.
• Measure out the ingredients carefully.
• Use the correct size tins (pans) and prepare them before you start combining the ingredients.

Parkin

The flavour of this dense and sticky cake will improve if it is stored in an airtight container for several days or a week before serving.

Makes 16–20 squares

300ml/½ pint/1¼ cups milk
225g/8oz/scant ⅔ cup golden (light corn) syrup
225g/8oz/scant ⅔ cup black treacle (molasses)
115g/4oz/½ cup butter or margarine, diced
50g/2oz/¼ cup soft dark brown sugar
450g/1lb/4 cups plain (all-purpose) flour
2.5ml/½ tsp bicarbonate of soda (baking soda)
6.5ml/1¼ tsp ground ginger
350g/12oz/3 cups medium oatmeal
1 egg, beaten
icing (confectioners') sugar, for dusting

I Preheat the oven to 180°C/350°F/Gas 4. Grease and line the base of a 20cm/8in square cake tin (pan).

2 Gently heat together the milk, syrup, treacle, butter or margarine and sugar in a pan, stirring until smooth. Do not allow the mixture to boil.

3 Stir together the flour, bicarbonate of soda, ginger and oatmeal.

4 Make a well in the centre, pour in the egg, then slowly pour in the warmed mixture, stirring to make a smooth batter.

5 Pour the batter into the tin and bake for about 45 minutes, until firm to the touch. Cool slightly in the tin, then cool completely on a wire rack. Cut into squares or thick slices and dust with icing sugar.

Cook's Tip

This traditional cake is made using the melted cakes method. Melted cakes have a satisfying dense, sticky texture created by using treacle (molasses) or golden (light corn) syrup. Baking powder or bicarbonate of soda (baking soda) are usually used to make melted cakes rise. Melted cakes store well and generally improve with keeping for a few days.

Apple Cake Energy 2436kcal/10244kJ; Protein 30.5g; Carbohydrate 368.6g, of which sugars 197.9g; Fat 103.7g, of which saturates 62.2g; Cholesterol 437mg; Calcium 495mg; Fibre 10.5g; Sodium 801mg.
Parkin Energy 273kcal/1152kJ; Protein 5.3g; Carbohydrate 50g, of which sugars 20.1g; Fat 7.1g, of which saturates 3.3g; Cholesterol 23mg; Calcium 127mg; Fibre 1.9g; Sodium 102mg.

Banana Ginger Parkin

The combination of banana and ginger gives a new slant to the traditional recipe for this delicious cake.

Makes 16–20 squares

200g/7oz/1¾ cups plain (all-purpose) flour
10ml/2 tsp bicarbonate of soda (baking soda)
10ml/2 tsp ground ginger
150g/5oz/1¼ cups medium oatmeal
50g/2oz/¼ cup muscovado sugar (molasses)
75g/3oz/6 tbsp sunflower margarine
150g/5oz/3 tbsp golden (light corn) syrup
1 egg, beaten
3 ripe bananas, mashed
75g/3oz/¾ cup icing (confectioners') sugar
preserved stem ginger, to decorate (optional)

1 Preheat the oven to 160°C/325°F/Gas 3. Grease and line an 18 × 28cm/7 × 11in cake tin (pan).

2 Sift together the flour, bicarbonate of soda and ginger in a bowl, then stir in the oatmeal.

3 Melt the sugar, margarine and syrup in a pan over a low heat, then stir into the flour mixture.

4 Beat the egg and mashed bananas into the flour mixture until thoroughly combined. Spoon the mixture into the prepared tin and bake for about 1 hour, or until firm to the touch.

5 Leave the cake to cool in the tin for 5 minutes, then turn it out on to a wire rack and allow it to cool completely.

6 If you want to keep the cake for a few months, wrap it in foil and put it in an airtight container without cutting it. If you want to eat it immediately, cut it into squares.

7 Make the icing when you want to serve the cake: sift the icing sugar into a bowl and stir in just enough water to make a smooth, runny icing. Drizzle the icing over each square of cake in a zigzag pattern and top with a piece of stem ginger, if you like.

Gooseberry Cake

This cake is delicious served warm with whipped cream.

Makes one 18cm/7in square cake

115g/4oz/½ cup butter
165g/5½oz/1⅓ cups self-raising (self-rising) flour
5ml/1 tsp baking powder
2 eggs, beaten
115g/4oz/generous ½ cup caster (superfine) sugar
5–10ml/1–2 tsp rose water
pinch of freshly grated nutmeg
115g/4oz jar gooseberries in syrup, drained, juice reserved
caster (superfine) sugar, to decorate
whipped cream, to serve

1 Preheat the oven to 180°C/350°F/Gas 4. Grease an 18cm/7in square cake tin (pan) and line the base and sides with baking parchment. Grease the paper.

2 Gently melt the butter in a pan, then transfer to a large bowl and allow to cool.

3 Sift together the flour and baking powder and add to the butter in the bowl.

4 Beat in the eggs, one at a time, the sugar, rose water and grated nutmeg, until you have a smooth batter.

5 Mix in 15–30ml/1–2 tbsp of the reserved gooseberry juice from the jar, then pour half of the batter mixture into the prepared tin. Sprinkle over the gooseberries and pour over the remaining batter mixture.

6 Bake for about 45 minutes, or until a skewer inserted into the centre of the cake comes out clean.

7 Leave in the tin for 5 minutes, then turn out on a wire rack, peel off the lining paper and allow to cool for a further 5 minutes.

8 Dredge with caster sugar and serve immediately with whipped cream, or leave the cake to cool completely before decorating.

Ginger Parkin Energy 157kcal/662kJ; Protein 2.4g; Carbohydrate 29.2g, of which sugars 15.8g; Fat 4.2g, of which saturates 0.7g; Cholesterol 10mg; Calcium 25mg; Fibre 1g; Sodium 57mg.
Gooseberry Cake Energy 2080kcal/8719kJ; Protein 30.1g; Carbohydrate 263.9g, of which sugars 138.2g; Fat 108.1g, of which saturates 63.3g; Cholesterol 626mg; Calcium 392mg; Fibre 7.3g; Sodium 857mg.

Pineapple Upside-down Cake

Canned pineapple rings make this a useful and unusual cake to make with a few ingredients that you might already have in the cupboard.

Makes one 25cm/10in round cake
115g/4oz/½ cup butter
200g/7oz/scant 1 cup soft dark
  brown sugar

450g/1lb canned pineapple
  slices, drained
4 eggs, separated
grated rind of 1 lemon
pinch of salt
115g/4oz/generous ½ cup caster
  (superfine) sugar
75g/3oz/⅔ cup plain
  (all-purpose) flour
5ml/1 tsp baking powder

1 Preheat the oven to 180°C/350°F/Gas 4. Melt the butter in a 25cm/10in ovenproof cast-iron frying pan. Then reserve 15ml/1 tbsp butter. Add the brown sugar to the pan and stir to blend. Place the pineapple slices on top in one layer. Set aside.

2 Whisk together the egg yolks, reserved butter and lemon rind until well blended. Set aside.

3 Beat the egg whites and salt until they form stiff peaks. Gradually fold in the caster sugar, then the egg yolk mixture.

4 Sift the flour and baking powder together. Carefully fold into the egg mixture in three batches.

5 Pour the mixture over the pineapple. Bake until a skewer inserted in the centre comes out clean, about 30 minutes.

6 While still hot, invert on to a serving plate. Serve hot or cold.

> **Variation**
> For an apricot cake, replace the pineapple slices with 225g/8oz/1¾ cups dried ready-to-eat apricots.

Upside-down Pear and Ginger Cake

This light spicy sponge, topped with glossy baked fruit and ginger, makes an excellent pudding.

Serves 6–8
900g/2lb can pear halves, drained
120ml/8 tbsp finely chopped
  preserved stem ginger
120ml/8 tbsp ginger syrup from
  the jar

175g/6oz/1½ cups self-raising
  (self-rising) flour
2.5ml/½ tsp baking powder
5ml/1 tsp ground ginger
175g/6oz/¾ cup soft light
  brown sugar
175g/6oz/¾ cup butter,
  softened
3 eggs, lightly beaten

1 Preheat the oven to 180°C/350°F/Gas 4. Base-line and grease a deep 20cm/8in round cake tin (pan).

2 Fill the hollow in each pear with half the chopped preserved stem ginger. Arrange, flat sides down, in the base of the cake tin, then spoon over half the ginger syrup.

3 Sift together the flour, baking powder and ground ginger. Stir in the sugar and butter, add the eggs and beat until creamy, about 1–2 minutes.

4 Spoon the mixture into the cake tin. Bake in the oven for 50 minutes, or until a skewer inserted in the centre of the cake comes out clean. Leave the cake in the tin for 5 minutes. Turn out on to a wire rack, peel off the lining paper and leave to cool completely.

5 Add the reserved ginger to the pear halves and drizzle over the remaining syrup.

> **Cook's Tip**
> Canned pears are ideal for this cake, but you can also core, peel and halve fresh pears, and then poach them until tender in a little white wine to cover with 50g/2oz/1½ cup sugar added.

Pineapple Cake Energy 2858kcal/12025kJ; Protein 35.7g; Carbohydrate 443g, of which sugars 385.9g; Fat 117.7g, of which saturates 66.3g; Cholesterol 1006mg; Calcium 443mg; Fibre 4.6g; Sodium 1003mg.
Pear and Ginger Cake Energy 433kcal/1818kJ; Protein 5g; Carbohydrate 61.4g, of which sugars 44.7g; Fat 20.4g, of which saturates 12g; Cholesterol 118mg; Calcium 66mg; Fibre 2.3g; Sodium 205mg.

American Carrot Cake

This light and spicy carrot cake has the traditional topping.

Makes one 20cm/8in round cake

250ml/8fl oz/1 cup corn oil
175g/6oz/scant 1 cup caster (superfine) sugar
3 eggs
175g/6oz/1½ cups plain (all-purpose) flour
7.5ml/1½ tsp baking powder
7.5ml/1½ tsp bicarbonate of soda (baking soda)
1.5ml/¼ tsp salt
7.5ml/1½ tsp ground cinnamon

a good pinch of freshly grated nutmeg
1.5ml/¼ tsp ground ginger
115g/4oz/1 cup chopped walnuts
225g/8oz/generous 1½ cups finely grated carrots
5ml/1 tsp vanilla extract
30ml/2 tbsp sour cream
8 tiny marzipan carrots, to decorate

For the frosting

175g/6oz/¾ cup full-fat soft cheese
25g/1oz/2 tbsp butter, softened
225g/8oz/2 cups icing (confectioners') sugar, sifted

1 Preheat the oven to 180°C/350°F/Gas 4. Grease and line two 20cm/8in loose-based round cake tins (pans).

2 Put the corn oil and sugar into a bowl and beat well. Add the eggs, one at a time, and beat thoroughly. Sift the flour, baking powder, bicarbonate of soda, salt, cinnamon, nutmeg and ginger into the bowl and beat well.

3 Fold in the chopped walnuts and grated carrots, and stir in the vanilla extract and sour cream.

4 Divide the mixture between the prepared cake tins and bake in the centre of the oven for about 65 minutes, or until a skewer inserted into the centre of the cakes comes out clean. Leave to cool in the tins on a wire rack. Meanwhile, beat all the frosting ingredients together until smooth.

5 Sandwich the cakes together with a little frosting. Spread the remaining frosting over the top and sides of the cake. Just before serving, decorate with the marzipan carrots.

Passion Cake

This cake is associated with Passion Sunday. The carrot and banana give it a rich, moist texture.

Makes one 20cm/8in round cake

200g/7oz/1¾ cups self-raising (self-rising) flour
10ml/2 tsp baking powder
5ml/1 tsp cinnamon
2.5ml/½ tsp freshly grated nutmeg
150g/5oz/10 tbsp butter, softened, or sunflower margarine
150g/5oz/generous 1 cup soft light brown sugar
grated rind of 1 lemon

2 eggs, beaten
2 carrots, coarsely grated
1 ripe banana, mashed
115g/4oz/¾ cup raisins
50g/2oz/½ cup chopped walnuts or pecan nuts
30ml/2 tbsp milk
6–8 walnuts, halved, to decorate
coffee crystal sugar, to decorate

For the frosting

200g/7oz/scant 1 cup cream cheese, softened
30g/1½oz/scant ⅓ cup icing (confectioners') sugar
juice of 1 lemon
grated rind of 1 orange

1 Line and grease a deep 20cm/8in round cake tin (pan). Preheat the oven to 180°C/350°F/Gas 4. Sift the flour, baking powder and spices into a bowl.

2 In another bowl, cream the butter or margarine and sugar with the lemon rind until it is light and fluffy, then beat in the eggs. Fold in the flour mixture, then the carrots, banana, raisins, chopped nuts and milk.

3 Spoon the mixture into the prepared cake tin, level the top and bake for about 1 hour, or until risen and the top is springy to the touch. Turn the tin upside down and allow the cake to cool in the tin for 30 minutes. Then turn out on to a wire rack and leave to cool completely. When cold, split the cake in half.

4 To make the frosting, cream the cheese with the icing sugar, lemon juice and orange rind, then sandwich the two halves of the cake together with half of the frosting. Spread the rest of the frosting on top and decorate with walnut halves and sugar.

Carrot Cake Energy 5897kcal/24604kJ; Protein 61.9g; Carbohydrate 576.8g, of which sugars 441.6g; Fat 387.8g, of which saturates 106.3g; Cholesterol 808mg; Calcium 911mg; Fibre 14.9g; Sodium 992mg.
Passion Cake Energy 4318kcal/18033kJ; Protein 50.9g; Carbohydrate 456.2g, of which sugars 300.8g; Fat 267.4g, of which saturates 144.1g; Cholesterol 890mg; Calcium 798mg; Fibre 14.7g; Sodium 1777mg.

Chocolate Banana Cake

Fresh fruit is especially good for making a moist cake mixture. Here is a delicious sticky chocolate cake, moist enough to eat without the icing if you want to cut down on the calories.

Serves 8
225g/8oz/2 cups self-raising (self-rising) flour
45ml/3 tbsp reduced-fat unsweetened cocoa powder
115g/4oz/½ cup soft light brown sugar

30ml/2 tbsp malt extract
30ml/2 tbsp golden (light corn) syrup
2 eggs, beaten
60ml/4 tbsp skimmed milk
60ml/4 tbsp sunflower oil
2 large ripe bananas

For the icing
175g/6oz/1½ cups icing (confectioners') sugar, sifted
30ml/2 tbsp reduced-fat unsweetened cocoa powder, sifted
15–30ml/1–2 tbsp warm water

1 Preheat the oven to 160°C/325°F/Gas 3. Line and grease a deep 20cm/8in round cake tin (pan). Sift the flour into a mixing bowl with the cocoa powder. Stir in the sugar.

2 Make a well in the centre of the dry ingredients and add the malt extract, golden syrup, eggs, milk and oil. Mix well.

3 Mash the bananas thoroughly and stir them into the mixture until thoroughly combined.

4 Spoon the cake mixture into the prepared tin and bake for 1–1¼ hours, or until the centre of the cake springs back when lightly pressed.

5 Remove from the tin and turn on to a wire rack to cool.

6 To make the icing, put the icing sugar and cocoa in a mixing bowl and gradually add enough water to make a mixture thick enough to coat the back of a wooden spoon.

7 Pour over the top of the cake and ease to the edges, allowing the icing to dribble down the sides.

Spiced Apple Cake

As grated apple and dates give this cake a natural sweetness, it may not be necessary to add all the sugar.

Serves 8
225g/8oz/2 cups self-raising (self-rising) wholemeal (whole-wheat) flour
5ml/1 tsp baking powder
10ml/2 tsp ground cinnamon

175g/6oz/1 cup chopped dates
75g/3oz/scant ½ cup soft light brown sugar
15ml/1 tbsp pear and apple spread
120ml/4fl oz/½ cup apple juice
2 eggs, beaten
90ml/6 tbsp sunflower oil
2 eating apples, cored and grated
15ml/1 tbsp chopped walnuts

1 Preheat the oven to 180°C/350°F/Gas 4. Line and grease a 20cm/8in deep round cake tin (pan).

2 Sift the flour, baking powder and cinnamon into a mixing bowl, then mix in the dates and make a well in the centre.

3 Mix some of the sugar with the pear and apple spread in a small bowl. Gradually stir in the apple juice.

4 Add to the dry ingredients with the eggs, oil and apples. Mix thoroughly. Taste and add the rest of the sugar if necessary.

5 Spoon into the prepared cake tin, sprinkle with the walnuts and bake for 60–65 minutes, or until a skewer inserted into the centre of the cake comes out clean.

6 Invert on a wire rack, remove the lining paper and leave to cool.

> ### Cook's Tip
> It is not necessary to peel the apples – the skin adds extra fibre and softens on cooking.

Banana Cake Energy 352kcal/1487kJ; Protein 6.5g; Carbohydrate 64.4g, of which sugars 41.9g; Fat 9.4g, of which saturates 2.3g; Cholesterol 48mg; Calcium 145mg; Fibre 2.3g; Sodium 233mg.
Apple Cake Energy 282kcal/1186kJ; Protein 4.9g; Carbohydrate 42.8g, of which sugars 21.3g; Fat 11.3g, of which saturates 1.5g; Cholesterol 48mg; Calcium 60mg; Fibre 1.6g; Sodium 22mg.

Irish Whiskey Cake

This moist rich fruit cake is drizzled with whiskey as soon as it comes out of the oven. It is high in fibre and full of flavour.

Serves 10

115g/4oz/³/4 cup sultanas
 (golden raisins)
115g/4oz/scant 1 cup raisins

115g/4oz/½ cup currants
115g/4oz/½ cup glacé
 (candied) cherries
175g/6oz/1¼ cups soft light
 brown sugar
300ml/½ pint/1¼ cups cold tea
1 egg, beaten
300g/11oz/2²/3 cups self-raising
 (self-rising) flour, sifted
45ml/3 tbsp Irish whiskey

1 Mix the sultanas, raisins, currants, cherries, sugar and tea in a large bowl. Leave to soak overnight until the tea has been absorbed.

2 Preheat the oven to 180°C/350°F/Gas 4. Line and grease a 1kg/2¼lb loaf tin (pan).

3 Add the egg and flour to the fruit mixture and beat thoroughly until well mixed.

4 Pour into the prepared tin and bake for 1½ hours or until a skewer inserted into the centre comes out clean.

5 Prick over the top of the cake with a skewer and drizzle over the whiskey while the cake is still hot.

6 Allow to stand for 5 minutes, then remove from the tin and cool completely on a wire rack.

Variation
For a tangy finish, drizzle with lemon icing. Mix the juice of 1 lemon with 225g/8oz/2 cup icing (confectioners') sugar and enough warm water for the icing to have a thin consistency. Drizzle the icing over the cooled cake and decorate with crystallized lemon slices, if you like.

Fruit and Nut Cake

A rich, fibrous fruit cake that matures with keeping. Omit the fruit and nut decoration from the top if you want to ice it for a Christmas cake.

Serves 12–14

175g/6oz/1½ cups self-raising
 (self-rising) wholemeal
 (whole-wheat) flour
175g/6oz/1½ cups self-raising
 (self-rising) white flour
10ml/2 tsp mixed (apple pie) spice

15ml/1 tbsp apple and
 apricot spread
45ml/3 tbsp clear honey
15ml/1 tbsp molasses
90ml/6 tbsp sunflower oil
175ml/6fl oz/¾ cup orange juice
2 eggs, beaten
675g/1½lb/4 cups luxury mixed
 dried fruit
115g/4oz/½ cup glacé (candied)
 cherries, halved
45ml/3 tbsp split almonds

1 Preheat the oven to 160°C/325°F/Gas 3. Line and grease a deep 20cm/8in cake tin (pan). Tie a band of newspaper around the outside of the tin and stand it on a pad of newspaper on a baking sheet.

2 Combine the flours in a mixing bowl. Stir in the mixed spice and make a well in the centre.

3 Put the apple and apricot spread in a small bowl. Gradually stir in the honey and molasses. Add to the bowl with the oil, orange juice, eggs and mixed fruit. Stir with a wooden spoon to mix thoroughly.

4 Scrape the mixture into the prepared tin and smooth the surface. Arrange the cherries and almonds in a decorative pattern over the top. Bake for 2 hours, or until a skewer inserted into the centre of the cake comes out clean. Turn on to a wire rack to cool, then remove the lining paper.

Cook's Tip
For a less elaborate cake, omit the cherries, chop the almonds roughly and sprinkle them over the top.

Strawberry Gateau

It is difficult to believe that a cake that tastes so delicious can be low fat. It is the perfect way to enjoy the first locally grown strawberries of the season.

Serves 6
2 eggs
75g/3oz/6 tbsp caster
 (superfine) sugar
grated rind of ½ orange
50g/2oz/½ cup plain
 (all-purpose) flour

For the filling
275g/10oz/1¼ cups low-fat
 soft cheese
grated rind of ½ orange
30ml/2 tbsp caster
 (superfine) sugar
60ml/4 tbsp reduced-fat fromage
 frais or crème fraîche
225g/8oz/2 cups strawberries,
 halved and chopped
25g/1oz/¼ cup chopped
 almonds, toasted

1 Preheat the oven to 190°C/375°F/Gas 5. Line a 30 × 20cm/12 × 8in Swiss roll tin (jelly roll pan) with baking parchment.

2 In a bowl, whisk the eggs, sugar and orange rind until thick and mousse-like, then lightly fold in the flour.

3 Turn into the prepared tin. Bake for 15–20 minutes, or until the surface is firm to the touch and golden.

4 Turn the cake out on to on a wire rack to cool. When cold, remove the lining paper.

5 Meanwhile, make the filling. In a bowl, mix the soft cheese with the grated orange rind, sugar and fromage frais until smooth. Divide the mixture between two bowls.

6 Add half the strawberries to one bowl. Cut the sponge horizontally into three equal pieces and sandwich together with the strawberry filling. Place the gateau on a serving plate.

7 Spread the plain filling over the top and sides of the cake. Press the toasted almonds over the sides and decorate the top with the remaining strawberry halves.

Tia Maria Gateau

A feather-light coffee sponge with a creamy liqueur-flavoured filling spiked with preserved stem ginger.

Serves 8
75g/3oz/¾ cup plain
 (all-purpose) flour
30ml/2 tbsp instant
 coffee powder
3 eggs
115g/4oz/½ cup caster
 (superfine) sugar

For the filling
175g/6oz/generous ¾ cup low-fat
 soft cheese
15ml/1 tbsp clear honey
15ml/1 tbsp Tia Maria
50g/2oz/⅓ cup preserved stem
 ginger, chopped

For the icing
225g/8oz/2 cups icing
 (confectioners') sugar, sifted
10ml/2 tsp coffee extract
5ml/1 tsp fat-reduced cocoa
coffee beans (optional)

1 Preheat the oven to 190°C/375°F/Gas 5. Line and grease a 20cm/8in round cake tin (pan). Sift the flour and coffee powder together into a bowl.

2 Whisk the eggs and sugar in a bowl until thick and mousse-like, then fold in the flour mixture lightly. Turn the mixture into the prepared tin. Bake for 30–35 minutes, or until firm and golden. Leave to cool on a wire rack.

3 To make the filling, mix the soft cheese with the honey in a bowl. Beat until smooth, then stir in the Tia Maria and preserved stem ginger. Split the cake in half horizontally and sandwich together with the Tia Maria filling.

4 To make the icing, mix the icing sugar and coffee extract in a bowl with enough water to make an icing which will coat the back of a wooden spoon. Pour three-quarters of the icing over the cake.

5 Stir the cocoa into the remaining icing, spoon it into a piping (icing) bag fitted with a writing nozzle and drizzle the mocha icing over the coffee icing. Decorate with coffee beans, if you like.

Strawberry Gateau Energy 305kcal/1288kJ; Protein 25.6g; Carbohydrate 35.7g, of which sugars 22.4g; Fat 7.6g, of which saturates 1.1g; Cholesterol 64mg; Calcium 163mg; Fibre 7.2g; Sodium 37mg.
Tia Maria Gateau Energy 247kcal/1050kJ; Protein 4.9g; Carbohydrate 54.7g, of which sugars 47.4g; Fat 2.5g, of which saturates 1.5g; Cholesterol 12mg; Calcium 65mg; Fibre 0.5g; Sodium 120mg.

Cinnamon and Apple Gateau

Make this lovely moist gateau as a guilt-free autumn teatime treat.

Serves 8
3 eggs
115g/4oz/^{1}/$_2$ cup caster
   (superfine) sugar
75g/3oz/^{3}/$_4$ cup plain
   (all-purpose) flour
5ml/1 tsp ground cinnamon

For the filling and topping
4 large eating apples
15ml/1 tbsp water
60ml/4 tbsp clear honey
75g/3oz/^{1}/$_2$ cup sultanas
   (golden raisins)
2.5ml/^{1}/$_2$ tsp ground cinnamon
350g/12oz/1^1/$_2$ cups low-fat
   soft cheese
60ml/4 tbsp reduced-fat fromage
   frais or low-fat cream cheese
10ml/2 tsp lemon juice

1 Preheat the oven to 190°C/375°F/Gas 5. Line and grease a 23cm/9in shallow round cake tin (pan). Whisk the eggs and sugar until thick, then sift the flour and cinnamon over the surface and carefully fold in with a large metal spoon.

2 Pour into the prepared tin and bake for 25–30 minutes, or until the cake springs back when lightly pressed. Leave on a wire rack to cool completely.

3 To make the filling, peel, core and slice three of the apples and cook them in a covered pan with the water and half the honey until softened. Add the sultanas and cinnamon, stir well, replace the lid and leave to cool.

4 Put the soft cheese in a bowl with the fromage frais, the remaining honey and half the lemon juice; beat until smooth. Split the sponge cake in half, place the bottom half on a plate and drizzle over any liquid from the apples.

5 Spread with two-thirds of the cheese mixture, then top with the apple filling. Fit the top of the cake in place.

6 Swirl the remaining filling over the top of the sponge. Quarter, core and slice the remaining apple, dip the slices in the remaining lemon juice and use to decorate the edges.

Lemon Chiffon Cake

Tangy lemon mousse makes a delicious filling in this light cake, which is surprisingly low in saturated fat.

Serves 8
1 lemon sponge cake mix
lemon glacé icing
shreds of blanched lemon rind

For the filling
2 eggs, separated
75g/3oz/6 tbsp caster
   (superfine) sugar
grated rind and juice of
   1 small lemon
20ml/4 tsp water
10ml/2 tsp powdered gelatine
120ml/4fl oz/^{1}/$_2$ cup reduced-fat
   fromage frais or crème fraîche

1 Preheat the oven to 180°C/350°F/Gas 4. Line and grease a 20cm/8in loose-based cake tin (pan).

2 Add the sponge mixture and bake for 20–25 minutes, or until firm and golden. Cool on a wire rack, then split the cake in half. Return the lower half of the cake to the clean cake tin and set aside.

3 To make the filling, whisk the egg yolks, sugar, lemon rind and juice in a bowl until thick, pale and creamy. In a grease-free bowl, whisk the egg whites until they form soft peaks.

4 Sprinkle the gelatine over the water in a heatproof bowl. When the gelatine has become spongy, place the bowl over a pan of simmering water and dissolve the gelatine, stirring occasionally. Cool slightly, then whisk into the yolk mixture. Fold in the fromage frais.

5 When the mixture begins to set, fold in a generous spoonful of the egg whites to lighten it, then fold in the remaining whites.

6 Spoon the lemon mousse over the sponge in the cake tin. Set the second layer of sponge on top and chill until set.

7 Carefully transfer the cake to a serving plate. Pour the glacé icing over the cake and spread it evenly to the edges. Decorate with the lemon shreds.

Apple Gateau Energy 239kcal/1010kJ; Protein 10.8g; Carbohydrate 39.9g, of which sugars 32.8g; Fat 5.8g, of which saturates 2.9g; Cholesterol 82mg; Calcium 97mg; Fibre 1.1g; Sodium 225mg.
Lemon Cake Energy 356kcal/1491kJ; Protein 6.7g; Carbohydrate 43.6g, of which sugars 29.8g; Fat 18.4g, of which saturates 4g; Cholesterol 118mg; Calcium 68mg; Fibre 0.6g; Sodium 227mg.

White Bread

There is nothing quite like the smell and taste of home-baked bread, eaten while still warm.

**Makes two 23 x 13cm/
9 x 5in loaves**
50ml/2fl oz/¼ cup
  lukewarm water
15ml/1 tbsp active dried yeast
30ml/2 tbsp caster
  (superfine) sugar
475ml/16fl oz/2 cups
  lukewarm milk
25g/1oz/2 tbsp butter or
  margarine, at room temperature
10ml/2 tsp salt
about 900g/2lb/8 cups strong
  white bread flour

1 Combine the water, yeast and 15ml/1 tbsp of the sugar in a measuring jug (cup) and leave for 15 minutes, or until frothy.

2 Pour the milk into a large bowl. Add the remaining sugar, the butter or margarine, and salt.

3 Stir in the yeast mixture, then stir in the flour, 150g/5oz/ 1¼ cups at a time, until a stiff dough is obtained.

4 Transfer the dough to a floured surface. Knead the dough until it is smooth and elastic, then place it in a large greased bowl, cover with clear film (plastic wrap), and leave to rise in a warm place until doubled in volume, about 2–3 hours.

5 Grease two 23 x 13cm/9 x 5in loaf tins (pans). Knock back (punch down) the dough and divide in half.

6 Form into loaf shapes and place in the tins, seam down. Cover and leave to rise again until almost doubled in volume, about 45 minutes. Meanwhile, preheat the oven to 190°C/ 375°F/Gas 5.

7 Bake the loaves until firm and brown, about 45–50 minutes. Turn out and tap the base of a loaf: if it sounds hollow the loaf is done. If necessary, return to the oven and bake for a few minutes longer. (Turn the loaf upside down in the tin if the top is done but the base is not.) Turn out and cool on a wire rack.

Braided Loaf

It doesn't take much effort to turn an ordinary dough mix into this work of art.

Makes one loaf
15ml/1 tbsp active dried yeast
5ml/1 tsp honey
250ml/8fl oz/1 cup
  lukewarm milk
50g/2oz/¼ cup butter, melted
425g/15oz/3⅔ cups strong
  white bread flour
5ml/1 tsp salt
1 egg, lightly beaten
1 egg yolk, beaten with
  5ml/1 tsp milk, to glaze

1 Combine the yeast, honey, milk and butter in a small bowl. Stir and leave for 15 minutes to dissolve and for the yeast to become frothy.

2 In a large bowl, mix together the flour and salt. Make a central well in the flour, and add the yeast mixture and egg. With a wooden spoon, stir from the centre, gradually incorporating the flour into the liquid, to obtain a rough dough.

3 Transfer the dough to a floured surface and knead until smooth and elastic. This will take about 10 minutes.

4 Place in a clean bowl, cover with clear film (plastic wrap) and leave to rise in a warm place until doubled in volume, about 1½ hours.

5 Grease a baking sheet. Punch down (knock back) the dough and divide into three equal pieces.

6 Roll each piece into a long thin strip. Begin braiding with the centre strip, tucking in the ends neatly when you reach the end of the braid. Cover loosely with clear film and leave to rise in a warm place for 30 minutes.

7 Meanwhile, preheat the oven to 190°C/375°F/Gas 5. Brush the bread with the egg and milk glaze and bake until it is golden, about 40–45 minutes. Turn the loaf out on to a wire rack to cool.

White Bread Energy 1796kcal/7623kJ; Protein 50.6g; Carbohydrate 376.6g, of which sugars 33.7g; Fat 20.2g, of which saturates 10g; Cholesterol 41mg; Calcium 925mg; Fibre 14g; Sodium 193mg.
Braided Loaf Energy 2033kcal/8584kJ; Protein 55g; Carbohydrate 348.4g, of which sugars 24.5g; Fat 56.4g, of which saturates 31.1g; Cholesterol 312mg; Calcium 933mg; Fibre 13.2g; Sodium 494mg.

Multigrain Bread

Try different flours, such as rye, cornmeal, buckwheat or barley, to replace the wheatgerm and the soya flour used here.

Makes two 21 x 12cm/ 8½ x 4½in loaves
15ml/1 tbsp active dried yeast
50ml/2fl oz/¼ cup lukewarm water
65g/2½oz/¾ cup rolled oats
475ml/16fl oz/2 cups milk
10ml/2 tsp salt
50ml/2fl oz/¼ cup oil
50g/2oz/¼ cup soft light
  brown sugar
30ml/2 tbsp honey
2 eggs, lightly beaten
25g/1oz wheatgerm
175g/6oz/1½ cups soya flour
350g/12oz/3 cups strong
  wholemeal (whole-wheat) flour
about 450g/1lb/4 cups strong
  white bread flour

1 Combine the yeast and water in a bowl, stir, and leave for 15 minutes to dissolve and for the yeast to become frothy. Place the oats in a large bowl. Boil the milk, then pour over the rolled oats. Stir in the salt, oil, sugar and honey. Leave until lukewarm.

2 Stir in the yeast mixture, eggs, wheatgerm, soya and wholemeal flours. Gradually stir in enough strong white bread flour to obtain a rough dough.

3 Transfer the dough to a floured surface and knead, adding flour if necessary, until smooth and elastic. This will take about 10 minutes. Return to a clean bowl, cover with clear film (plastic wrap) and leave to rise in a warm place until doubled in volume, about 2½ hours.

4 Grease two 21 x 12cm/8½ x 4½in loaf tins (pans). Knock back (punch down) the risen dough and knead briefly. Then divide the dough into quarters. Roll each quarter into a cylinder 4cm/1½in thick. Twist together two cylinders and place in a tin; repeat for the remaining cylinders. Cover with clear film and leave to rise until doubled in volume again, about 1 hour. Meanwhile, preheat the oven to 190°C/375°F/Gas 5.

5 Bake until the bases sound hollow when tapped lightly, about 45–50 minutes. Turn out and cool on a wire rack.

Wholemeal Bread

A simple wholesome bread to be enjoyed by the entire family at any time.

Makes one 23 x 13cm/ 9 x 5in loaf
525g/1lb 5oz/5¼ cups strong
  wholemeal (whole-wheat)
  bread flour
10ml/2 tsp salt
20ml/4 tsp active dried yeast
450ml/¾ pint/scant 2 cups
  lukewarm water
30ml/2 tbsp honey
30ml/2 tbsp oil
40g/1½oz wheatgerm
milk, to glaze

1 Warm the flour and salt in a bowl in the oven at its lowest setting for 10 minutes.

2 Meanwhile, combine the yeast with half of the water in a bowl and leave to dissolve and for the yeast to become frothy.

3 Make a central well in the flour. Pour in the yeast mixture, the remaining water, honey, oil and wheatgerm. Stir in the flour from the centre, incorporating it as you go, until smooth.

4 Grease a 23 x 13cm/9 x 5in loaf tin (pan). Knead the dough just enough to shape into a loaf. Put it in the tin and cover with clear film (plastic wrap). Leave in a warm place until the dough is about 2.5cm/1in higher than the tin rim, about 1 hour.

5 Preheat the oven to 200°C/400°F/Gas 6. Brush the loaf with milk, and bake until the base sounds hollow when tapped, about 35–40 minutes. Cool on a wire rack.

Cook's Tip
For all yeast recipes use strong bread flours and not plain (all-purpose) or self-raising (self-rising) flours. Strong bread flours have a high gluten content, which is important to allow the yeast to rise well. Breads made with strong flours are light and have an airy crumb. Soda breads or any other breads not made with yeast do not use strong flours, however.

Wholemeal Energy 1997kcal/8459kJ; Protein 77.4g; Carbohydrate 361g, of which sugars 25.1g; Fat 37.2g, of which saturates 4.7g; Cholesterol 0mg; Calcium 222mg; Fibre 53.5g; Sodium 19mg.
Multigrain Energy 2266kcal/9595kJ; Protein 104.9g; Carbohydrate 389.3g, of which sugars 69.5g; Fat 43.1g, of which saturates 8g; Cholesterol 204mg; Calcium 944mg; Fibre 38.7g; Sodium 211mg.

Country Bread

A filling bread made with a mixture of wholemeal and white flour.

Makes two loaves

350g/12oz/3 cups strong
   wholemeal (whole-wheat)
   bread flour
350g/12oz/3 cups plain
   (all-purpose) flour
150g/5oz/1¼ cups strong white
   bread flour
20ml/4 tsp salt

50g/2oz/¼ cup butter,
   at room temperature
475ml/16fl oz/2 cups
   lukewarm milk

For the starter

15ml/1 tbsp active dried yeast
250ml/8fl oz/1 cup
   lukewarm water
150g/5oz/1¼ cups plain
   (all-purpose) flour
1.5ml/¼ tsp caster
   (superfine) sugar

1 To make the starter, mix the yeast, water, plain flour and sugar in a bowl. Cover and leave in a warm place for 2–3 hours.

2 Place the flours, salt and butter in a food processor and process until just blended, about 1–2 minutes.

3 Stir together the milk and starter, then slowly pour into the processor, with the motor running, until the mixture forms a dough. Knead the dough until smooth. This will take about 10 minutes.

4 Place in an ungreased bowl, cover with clear film (plastic wrap), and leave to rise in a warm place until doubled in size, about 1½ hours. Knock back (punch down) and then return to the bowl and leave until tripled in size, about 1½ hours.

5 Grease a baking sheet. Divide the dough in half. Cut off one-third of the dough from each half and shape all the pieces into balls. Top each large ball with a small ball and press the centre with the handle of a wooden spoon to secure. Cover with oiled clear film, slash the top, and leave the dough to rise once again.

6 Preheat the oven to 200°C/400°F/Gas 6. Dust the loaves with flour and bake until browned and the bases sound hollow when tapped, 45–50 minutes. Cool on a wire rack.

Oatmeal Bread

A healthy, rustic-looking bread made with rolled oats as well as flour.

Makes two loaves

475ml/16fl oz/2 cups milk
25g/1oz/2 tbsp butter
50g/2oz/¼ cup cup soft dark
   brown sugar

10ml/2 tsp salt
15ml/1 tbsp active dried yeast
50ml/2fl oz/¼ cup
   lukewarm water
400g/14oz/4 cups rolled oats
675–900g/1½–2lb/6–8 cups
   strong white bread flour

1 Put the milk in a small pan and bring to boiling point. Quickly remove from the heat and stir in the butter, brown sugar and salt. Leave the mixture to cool until lukewarm.

2 Combine the yeast and warm water in a large bowl and leave for about 15 minutes until frothy.

3 Stir in the milk mixture. Add 275g/10oz/3 cups of the rolled oats and enough flour to obtain a soft dough.

4 Transfer the dough to a floured surface and knead until smooth and elastic.

5 Place in a greased bowl, cover with clear film (plastic wrap) and leave until doubled in volume, about 2–3 hours.

6 Grease a large baking sheet. Transfer the dough to a lightly floured surface and divide in half. Shape into rounds.

7 Place on the baking sheet, cover with a dish towel or oiled clear film and leave to rise until doubled in volume, about 1 hour.

8 Preheat the oven to 200°C/400°F/Gas 6. Score the tops of the loaves and sprinkle with the remaining oats.

9 Bake until the bases sound hollow when tapped, about 45–50 minutes. Turn out on to wire racks to cool.

Country Bread Energy 1760kcal/7482kJ; Protein 60.9g; Carbohydrate 375.5g, of which sugars 19.7g; Fat 12.1g, of which saturates 3.7g; Cholesterol 14mg; Calcium 807mg; Fibre 25.8g; Sodium 2082mg.
Oatmeal Bread Energy 2254kcal/9556kJ; Protein 64.8g; Carbohydrate 445.2g, of which sugars 42.4g; Fat 36.1g, of which saturates 9.8g; Cholesterol 41mg; Calcium 883mg; Fibre 24.1g; Sodium 256mg.

Caraway Rye Bread

To bring out the flavour of the caraway seeds, toast them lightly in the oven first, if you like.

Makes one loaf
200g/7oz/scant 1¾ cups
  rye flour
475ml/16fl oz/2 cups
  boiling water
120ml/4fl oz/½ cup black
  treacle (molasses)
65g/2½oz/5 tbsp butter,
  cut into pieces
15ml/1 tbsp salt
30ml/2 tbsp caraway seeds
15ml/1 tbsp active dried yeast
120ml/4fl oz/½ cup
  lukewarm water
about 850g/1lb 14oz/7½ cups
  strong white bread flour
semolina or flour, for dusting

1 Mix the rye flour, boiling water, treacle, butter, salt and caraway seeds in a large bowl. Leave to cool.

2 In another bowl, mix the yeast and lukewarm water and leave to dissolve and for the yeast to become frothy.

3 Stir into the rye flour mixture. Stir in just enough strong white bread flour to obtain a stiff dough. If it becomes too stiff to mix with the spoon, stir with your hands. Transfer to a floured surface and knead until the dough is no longer sticky and is smooth and shiny. This will take about 10 minutes.

4 Place in a greased bowl, cover with clear film (plastic wrap), and leave in a warm place until doubled in volume, about 1½ hours.

5 Knock back (punch down) the dough, cover, and leave to rise again for 30 minutes.

6 Preheat the oven to 180°C/350°F/Gas 4. Dust a baking sheet with semolina or flour.

7 Shape the dough into a ball. Place on the sheet and score several times across the top. Bake until the base sounds hollow when tapped, about 40 minutes. Cool on a wire rack.

Rye Bread

Rye bread is popular in Northern Europe and makes an excellent base for open sandwiches.

Makes 2 loaves, each serving 10
350g/12oz/3 cups strong
  wholemeal (whole-wheat) flour
225g/8oz/2 cups rye flour
115g/4oz/1 cup strong white
  bread flour
7.5ml/1½ tsp salt
1 sachet easy-blend (rapid-rise)
  dried yeast
30ml/2 tbsp caraway seeds
475ml/16fl oz/2 cups
  hand-hot water
30ml/2 tbsp molasses
30ml/2 tbsp sunflower oil

1 Grease a baking sheet. Put the flours in a bowl with the salt and yeast. Set aside 5ml/1 tsp of the caraway seeds and add the remainder to the bowl. Mix well, then make a well in the centre.

2 Add the water to the bowl with the molasses and oil. Stir from the centre outwards, gradually incorporating the flour and mixing to a soft dough, and adding a little extra water if necessary.

3 Turn the dough on to a floured surface and knead for 5 minutes until smooth and elastic. Divide the dough in half and shape into two 23cm/9in long oval loaves.

4 Flatten the loaves slightly and place them on the prepared baking sheet. Brush them with water and sprinkle with the remaining caraway seeds. Cover and leave in a warm place until doubled in size, about 1½ hours. Meanwhile, preheat the oven to 220°C/425°F/Gas 7.

5 Bake the loaves for 30 minutes, or until they sound hollow when tapped underneath. Allow to cool on a wire rack.

Cook's Tip
Using warm rather than cold liquid helps the yeast to start working, as it is a living organism that thrives in warm and moist conditions.

Rye Bread Energy 127kcal/540kJ; Protein 3.7g; Carbohydrate 25.7g, of which sugars 1.7g; Fat 1.8g, of which saturates 0.2g; Cholesterol 0mg; Calcium 19mg; Fibre 3.1g; Sodium 5mg.
Caraway Rye Bread Energy 4323kcal/18332kJ; Protein 98.1g; Carbohydrate 893.3g, of which sugars 93.3g; Fat 64.4g, of which saturates 33.6g; Cholesterol 128mg; Calcium 1926mg; Fibre 49.8g; Sodium 6502mg.

Austrian Three-Grain Bread

A mixture of grains gives this close-textured bread a delightful nutty flavour.

Makes 1 large loaf
225g/8oz/2 cups strong white
  bread flour
7.5ml/1½ tsp salt
225g/8oz/2 cups malted
  brown flour
225g/8oz/2 cups rye flour
75g/3oz/½ cup medium oatmeal
1 sachet easy-blend (rapid-rise)
  dried yeast
45ml/3 tbsp sunflower seeds
30ml/2 tbsp linseeds
475ml/16fl oz/2 cups
  hand-hot water
30ml/2 tbsp malt extract

1 Sift the plain flour and salt into a mixing bowl and add the remaining flours, oatmeal, yeast and sunflower seeds. Set aside 5ml/1 tsp of the linseeds and add the rest to the flour mixture. Make a well in the centre.

2 Add the water to the bowl with the malt extract. Gradually incorporate the flour and mix to a soft dough, adding extra water if necessary.

3 Flour a baking sheet. Turn the dough on to a floured surface and knead for 5 minutes, or until smooth and elastic.

4 Divide it in half. Roll each half into a sausage about 30cm/12in in length. Twist the two pieces together, dampen each end and press together firmly.

5 Lift the loaf on to the prepared baking sheet. Brush with water, sprinkle with the remaining linseeds and cover loosely with clear film (plastic wrap) (balloon it to trap the air inside). Leave in a warm place until doubled in size, about 1½ hours. Meanwhile, preheat the oven to 220°C/425°F/Gas 7.

6 Bake the bread for 10 minutes, then lower the oven temperature to 200°C/400°F/Gas 6 and cook for 20 minutes more, or until the loaf sounds hollow when tapped underneath.

7 Transfer the cooked loaf to a wire rack to cool completely.

Sesame Seed Bread

This delicious bread with its nutty flavour breaks into individual rolls. It is ideal for entertaining.

Makes one 23cm/9in loaf
10ml/2 tsp active dried yeast
300ml/½ pint/1¼ cups
  lukewarm water
200g/7oz/1¾ cups strong white
  bread flour
200g/7oz/scant 1¾ cups strong
  wholemeal (whole-wheat)
  bread flour
10ml/2 tsp salt
65g/2½oz/5 tbsp toasted
  sesame seeds
milk, to glaze
30ml/2 tbsp sesame seeds,
  for sprinkling

1 Combine the yeast and 75ml/5 tbsp of the water in a small bowl and leave to dissolve and for the yeast to become frothy.

2 Mix the flours and salt in a large bowl. Make a central well in the flour and pour in the yeast and water. Stir from the centre to obtain a rough dough.

3 Transfer to a floured surface and knead until smooth and elastic. This will take about 10 minutes. Return to the bowl and cover with clear film (plastic wrap). Leave in a warm place until the dough has doubled in size, about 1½–2 hours.

4 Grease a 23cm/9in round cake tin (pan). Knock back (punch down) the dough and knead in the sesame seeds.

5 Divide the dough into 16 balls and place in the tin. Cover with clear film (plastic wrap) and leave in a warm place until risen above the rim, about 1½ hours.

6 Preheat the oven to 220°C/425°F/Gas 7. Brush the loaf with milk and sprinkle with the sesame seeds. Bake for 15 minutes. Lower the heat to 190°C/375°F/Gas 5 and bake until the base sounds hollow when tapped, about 30 minutes. Turn the loaf out on a wire rack and leave to cool before breaking into individual rolls and serving.

Austrian Energy 3076kcal/13051kJ; Protein 92.2g; Carbohydrate 592g, of which sugars 32.2g; Fat 54.1g, of which saturates 5.2g; Cholesterol 0mg; Calcium 808mg; Fibre 57.3g; Sodium 126mg.
Sesame Seed Energy 1691kcal/7142kJ; Protein 56g; Carbohydrate 283.8g, of which sugars 7.5g; Fat 44.7g, of which saturates 6.4g; Cholesterol 0mg; Calcium 793mg; Fibre 29.3g; Sodium 3955mg.

Spiral Herb Bread

When you slice this unusual loaf, its herbal secret is revealed inside.

Makes two 23 x 13cm/ 9 x 5in loaves
30ml/2 tbsp active dried yeast
600ml/1 pint/2½ cups
   lukewarm water
30ml/2 tbsp caster
   (superfine) sugar
425g/15oz/3⅔ cups strong white
   bread flour

500g/1¼lb/5 cups strong
   wholemeal (whole-wheat)
   bread flour
15ml/1 tbsp salt
25g/1oz/2 tbsp butter
a large bunch of parsley,
   finely chopped
a bunch of spring onions
   (scallions), chopped
1 garlic clove, finely chopped
1 egg, lightly beaten
milk, for glazing
salt and ground black pepper

1 Combine the yeast and 50ml/2fl oz/¼ cup of the water with the sugar, stir and leave for 15 minutes to dissolve.

2 Combine the flours and salt in a large bowl. Make a central well and pour in the yeast mixture and the remaining water. With a wooden spoon, stir to a rough dough. Transfer to a floured surface; knead until smooth. Return to the bowl, cover with clear film (plastic wrap), and leave until doubled in size.

3 Meanwhile, combine the butter, parsley, spring onions and garlic in a large frying pan. Cook over a low heat, stirring, until softened. Season and set aside.

4 Grease two 23 x 13cm/9 x 5in loaf tins (pans). When the dough has risen, cut in half and roll each half into a rectangle 35 x 23cm/14 x 9in. Brush with the beaten egg and spread with the herb mixture. Roll up to enclose the filling, and pinch the short ends to seal. Place in the tins, seam-sides down. Cover and leave in a warm place until the dough rises above the tin rims, about 1½ hours.

5 Preheat the oven to 190°C/375°F/Gas 5. Brush the loaves with milk and bake until the bases sound hollow when tapped, about 55 minutes. Cool on a wire rack.

Olive and Oregano Bread

Fresh herbs are fabulous in loaves. This is an excellent accompaniment to all salads and is very good with grilled (broiled) goat's cheese.

Serves 8–10
15ml/1 tbsp olive oil
1 onion, chopped
450g/1lb/4 cups strong white
   bread flour
10ml/2 tsp easy-blend (rapid-rise)
   dried yeast

5ml/1 tsp salt
1.5ml/¼ tsp ground
   black pepper
50g/2oz/½ cup pitted black
   olives, roughly chopped
15ml/1 tbsp black olive paste
15ml/1 tbsp chopped
   fresh oregano
15ml/1 tbsp chopped
   fresh parsley
300ml/½ pint/1¼ cups
   hand-hot water

1 Lightly oil a baking sheet. Heat the olive oil in a frying pan and fry the onion until golden brown.

2 Sift the flour into a mixing bowl. Add the yeast, salt and pepper. Make a well in the centre.

3 Add the fried onion (with the oil), the olives, olive paste, chopped oregano and parsley, and the water. Stir from the centre outwards and gradually incorporate the flour. Mix to a soft dough, adding a little extra water if necessary.

4 Turn the dough on to a floured surface and knead for 5 minutes until smooth and elastic.

5 Shape into a 20cm/8in round and place on the baking sheet.

6 Using a sharp knife, make criss-cross cuts over the top, cover and leave in a warm place until doubled in size, about 1½ hours. Preheat the oven to 220°C/425°F/Gas 7.

7 Bake the olive and oregano loaf for 10 minutes, then lower the oven temperature to 200°C/400°F/Gas 6. Bake for 20 minutes more, or until the loaf sounds hollow when tapped underneath. Cool on a wire rack.

Oregano Bread Energy 172kcal/727kJ; Protein 4.4g; Carbohydrate 35.4g, of which sugars 1g; Fat 2.3g, of which saturates 0.4g; Cholesterol 0mg; Calcium 68mg; Fibre 1.7g; Sodium 134mg.
Spiral Bread Energy 1726kcal/7323kJ; Protein 58.3g; Carbohydrate 345.9g, of which sugars 10.3g; Fat 21.9g, of which saturates 8.6g; Cholesterol 122mg; Calcium 465mg; Fibre 30.6g; Sodium 3077mg.

Prosciutto and Parmesan Bread

This nourishing bread can be made very quickly, and makes a delicious meal when served with a tomato and feta cheese salad.

Serves 8
225g/8oz/2 cups self-raising (self-rising) wholemeal (whole-wheat) flour
225g/8oz/2 cups self-raising (self-rising) flour

5ml/1 tsp salt
5ml/1 tsp ground black pepper
75g/3oz prosciutto, chopped
30ml/2 tbsp chopped fresh parsley
25g/1oz/2 tbsp freshly grated Parmesan cheese
45ml/3 tbsp Meaux mustard
350ml/12fl oz/1½ cups buttermilk
skimmed milk, to glaze

1 Preheat the oven to 200°C/400°F/Gas 6 and lightly flour a baking sheet.

2 Put the wholemeal flour in a bowl and sift in the plain flour, salt and pepper. Stir in the ham and parsley. Set aside about half of the grated Parmesan cheese and add the rest to the flour mixture. Make a well in the centre.

3 Mix the mustard and buttermilk in a jug (pitcher), pour into the bowl and quickly mix to a soft dough.

4 Turn on to a well-floured surface and knead very briefly. Shape into an oval loaf and place on the baking sheet.

5 Brush the loaf with milk, sprinkle with the reserved Parmesan cheese and bake for 25–30 minutes, or until golden brown. Cool on a wire rack.

> **Cook's Tip**
> *When chopping the ham, sprinkle it with flour so that it does not stick together. Do not knead the mixture as for a yeast dough, or it will become tough. It should be mixed quickly and kneaded very briefly before shaping.*

Spinach and Bacon Bread

This bread is so tasty that it is a good idea to make double the quantity and freeze some of the loaves.

Makes 2 loaves, each serving 8
15ml/1 tbsp olive oil
1 onion, chopped
115g/4oz rindless smoked bacon rashers (strips), chopped
675g/1½lb/6 cups plain

(all-purpose) flour
7.5ml/1½ tsp salt
2.5ml/½ tsp freshly grated nutmeg
1 sachet easy-blend (rapid-rise) dried yeast
475ml/16fl oz/2 cups hand-hot water
225g/8oz chopped spinach, thawed if frozen
25g/1oz/¼ cup grated reduced-fat Cheddar cheese

1 Lightly oil two 23cm/9in cake tins (pans).

2 Heat the oil in a frying pan and fry the onion and bacon for 10 minutes, or until golden brown.

3 Sift the flour, salt and grated nutmeg into a mixing bowl, add the yeast and make a well in the centre. Add the water.

4 Tip in the fried bacon and onion, with the oil it was cooked in, then add the well-drained thawed spinach. Stir from the centre outwards, gradually incorporating the flour, and mix to a soft dough.

5 Turn the dough on to a floured surface and knead for 5 minutes until smooth and elastic. Divide the mixture in half. Shape each half into a ball, flatten slightly and place in a prepared tin, pressing the dough so that it extends to the edges.

6 Mark each loaf into six wedges and sprinkle with the cheese. Cover loosely with oiled clear film (plastic wrap) and leave in a warm place until each loaf has doubled in size, about 1½ hours. Meanwhile, preheat the oven to 200°C/400°F/Gas 6.

7 Bake the loaves for 25–30 minutes, or until they sound hollow when tapped underneath. Leave on a wire rack to cool completely.

Spinach and Bacon Energy 160kcal/680kJ; Protein 5.8g; Carbohydrate 32.6g, of which sugars 1.2g; Fat 1.6g, of which saturates 0.3g; Cholesterol 1mg; Calcium 98mg; Fibre 1.7g; Sodium 216mg.
Prosciutto and Parmesan Energy 229kcal/972kJ; Protein 11.1g; Carbohydrate 42.4g, of which sugars 3.5g; Fat 2.9g, of which saturates 1g; Cholesterol 10mg; Calcium 146mg; Fibre 3.4g; Sodium 334mg.

Rosemary Bread

Dill Bread

Tasty herb breads such as this are expensive to buy ready-made – and hard to find – and they never taste as good as home-made.

Makes two loaves
20ml/4 tsp active dried yeast
475ml/16fl oz/2 cups
   lukewarm water
30ml/2 tbsp caster
   (superfine) sugar
1.05kg/2lb 5½oz/scant 9½ cups
   strong white bread flour
½ onion, chopped
60ml/4 tbsp oil
a large bunch of dill,
   finely chopped
2 eggs, lightly beaten
150g/5oz/⅔ cup cottage cheese
20ml/4 tsp salt
milk, to glaze

1 Mix together the yeast, water and sugar in a large bowl and leave for 15 minutes to dissolve and for the yeast to become frothy. Stir in about half of the flour. Cover and leave to rise in a warm place for 45 minutes.

2 In a frying pan, cook the onion in 15ml/1 tbsp of the oil until soft, about 5 minutes. Set aside to cool, then stir into the yeast mixture.

3 Stir the dill, eggs, cottage cheese, salt and the remaining oil into the yeast. Gradually add the remaining flour until the dough is too stiff to stir.

4 Transfer to a floured surface and knead until smooth and elastic. This will take about 10 minutes. Place in a bowl, cover with clear film (plastic wrap) and leave to rise until doubled in volume, about 1–1½ hours.

5 Grease a large baking sheet. Cut the dough in half and shape into two rounds. Place on the sheet and leave to rise in a warm place for 30 minutes.

6 Preheat the oven to 190°C/375°F/Gas 5. Score the tops of the loaves, brush with the milk to glaze and bake until browned, about 50 minutes. Transfer to a wire rack to cool.

Sliced thinly, this herb bread is delicious with cheese or soup for a light meal.

**Makes one 23 x 13cm/
9 x 5in loaf**
1 sachet easy-blend (rapid-rise)
   dried yeast
175g/6oz/1½ cups strong wholemeal
   (whole-wheat) bread flour
175g/6oz/1½ cups self-raising
   (self-rising) flour
25g/1oz/2 tbsp butter
50ml/2fl oz/¼ cup warm water
250ml/8fl oz/1 cup milk,
   at room temperature
15ml/1 tbsp sugar
5ml/1 tsp salt
15ml/1 tbsp sesame seeds
15ml/1 tbsp dried chopped onion
15ml/1 tbsp fresh rosemary
   leaves
115g/4oz/1 cup cubed
   Cheddar cheese
rosemary leaves and coarse salt,
   to decorate

1 Mix the yeast with the wholemeal and self-raising flours in a large mixing bowl. Melt the butter in a small pan, then stir the warm water, milk, sugar, butter, salt, sesame seeds, onion and rosemary into the flour.

2 Knead thoroughly until quite smooth. This will take about 10 minutes. Flatten the dough, then add the cheese cubes. Knead them in until they are well combined.

3 Place the dough in a large clean bowl. Cover the bowl with a dish towel or clear film (plastic wrap) and put it in a warm place for 1½ hours, or until the dough has doubled in size.

4 Grease a 23 x 13cm/9 x 5in loaf tin (pan) with butter. Knock back (punch down) the dough and shape it into a loaf.

5 Place in the tin, cover with the dish towel or oiled clear film and leave for about 1 hour, or until doubled in size. Preheat the oven to 190°C/375°F/Gas 5.

6 Bake for 30 minutes. Cover the loaf with foil for the last 5–10 minutes of baking. Turn the bread out on to a wire rack to cool. Garnish with some rosemary leaves and coarse salt sprinkled on top.

Dill Bread Energy 2207kcal/9346kJ; Protein 65.5g; Carbohydrate 428.3g, of which sugars 27.6g; Fat 37.4g, of which saturates 6.9g; Cholesterol 202mg; Calcium 874mg; Fibre 16.7g; Sodium 313mg.
Rosemary Bread Energy 1999kcal/8422kJ; Protein 77.3g; Carbohydrate 280.2g, of which sugars 37.4g; Fat 68.7g, of which saturates 41.5g; Cholesterol 180mg; Calcium 1489mg; Fibre 22g; Sodium 3069mg.

Focaccia

This Italian flatbread makes a delicious snack with olives and feta cheese.

Serves 8

450g/1lb/4 cups strong white
    bread flour
5ml/1 tsp salt
1.5ml/1/4 tsp ground black pepper
10ml/2 tsp easy-blend (rapid-
    rise) dried yeast
a pinch of sugar

300ml/1/2 pint/11/4 cups
    hand-hot water
15ml/1 tbsp pesto
115g/4oz/2/3 cup pitted black
    olives, chopped
25g/1oz/1/2 cup drained sun-
    dried tomatoes in oil, chopped,
    plus 15ml/1 tbsp oil from
    the jar
5ml/1 tsp coarse sea salt
5ml/1 tsp chopped
    fresh rosemary

1 Lightly oil a 30 × 20cm/12 × 8in Swiss roll tin (jelly roll pan). Sift the flour, salt and pepper into a bowl. Add the yeast and sugar, and make a well in the centre.

2 Add the water with the pesto, olives and sun-dried tomatoes to the dry ingredients (reserve the oil). Mix to a soft dough, adding a little extra water if necessary. Turn on to a floured surface and knead for 5 minutes until smooth and elastic.

3 Roll into a rectangle measuring 33 × 23cm/13 × 9in. Drape over the rolling pin and place in the prepared tin. Leave to rise until doubled in size, about 1 1/2 hours. Meanwhile, preheat the oven to 220°C/425°F/Gas 7.

4 Using your fingertips, make indentations all over the dough. Brush with the oil from the sun-dried tomatoes, then sprinkle over the salt and chopped rosemary. Bake for 20–25 minutes, or until golden. Remove to a wire rack and serve warm.

> **Variation**
> *Try adding 15ml/1 tbsp fresh chopped sage and half a chopped onion to the dough and the same again sprinkled over the top before baking.*

Rosemary Focaccia

Italian flat bread is easy to make using a packet mix. Additions include olives and sun-dried tomatoes.

Makes two loaves

450g/1lb packet white bread mix

60ml/4 tbsp extra virgin olive oil
10ml/2 tsp dried rosemary, crushed
8 sun-dried tomatoes, chopped
12 black olives, pitted and chopped
200ml/7fl oz/scant 1 cup
    lukewarm water
sea salt flakes, for sprinkling

1 Following the instructions on the pack, combine the bread mix with half the oil, the rosemary, tomatoes, olives and enough water to form a firm dough.

2 Knead the dough on a lightly floured surface for about 5 minutes.

3 Return to the mixing bowl and cover with a piece of oiled clear film (plastic wrap). Leave the dough to rise in a warm place until doubled in size, about 1 hour.

4 Meanwhile, lightly grease two baking sheets and preheat the oven to 220°C/425°F/Gas 7.

5 Knock back (punch down) the dough and knead again. Divide into two and shape into flat rounds. Place on the baking sheet, and make indentations with your fingertips. Trickle over the remaining olive oil and sprinkle with sea salt flakes.

6 Bake the focaccia for 12–15 minutes until golden brown and cooked. Turn out on to wire racks to cool. This bread is best eaten slightly warm.

> **Cook's Tip**
> *A bread mix is quick but you can also make focaccia dough by mixing 500g/1lb/3 cups strong white bread flour with 5ml/1 tsp salt and 5ml/1 tsp easy-blend (rapid-rise) yeast. Then follow the recipe as above.*

Focaccia Energy 230kcal/973kJ; Protein 6.3g; Carbohydrate 44.2g, of which sugars 1.3g; Fat 4.3g, of which saturates 0.9g; Cholesterol 2mg; Calcium 111mg; Fibre 2.3g; Sodium 353mg.
Rosemary Focaccia Energy 1001kcal/4225kJ; Protein 22.4g; Carbohydrate 177.7g, of which sugars 6.2g; Fat 27.2g, of which saturates 4g; Cholesterol 0mg; Calcium 334mg; Fibre 8.1g; Sodium 505mg.

81

BREADS

Saffron Focaccia

A dazzling yellow bread that is both light in texture and distinctive in flavour. The olive oil drizzled over the top makes the bread moist and it keeps well.

Makes one loaf
a pinch of saffron threads
150ml/1/4 pint/2/3 cup boiling water
225g/8oz/2 cups strong white
  bread flour
2.5ml/1/2 tsp salt
5ml/1 tsp easy-blend (rapid-rise)
  dried yeast
15ml/1 tbsp olive oil

For the topping
2 garlic cloves, sliced
1 red onion, cut into thin wedges
rosemary sprigs
12 black olives, pitted and
  coarsely chopped
15ml/1 tbsp olive oil

1 Place the saffron in a heatproof jug (pitcher) and pour in the boiling water. Leave to infuse (steep) until lukewarm.

2 Place the flour, salt, yeast and olive oil in a food processor. Turn on and gradually add the saffron and its liquid. Process until the dough forms a ball. Alternatively, use your hands to incorporate the liquid into the flour.

3 Turn out on to a floured surface and knead for 10–15 minutes. Place in a bowl, cover with clear film (plastic wrap) and leave to rise until doubled in size, about 30–40 minutes.

4 Knock back (punch down) the dough and roll into an oval shape about 1cm/1/2in thick. Place on a lightly greased baking sheet and leave to rise for 30 minutes.

5 Preheat the oven to 200°C/400°F/Gas 6. With your fingers, press indentations over the surface of the bread.

6 To make the topping cover the dough with the sliced garlic, onion wedges, rosemary sprigs and chopped olives.

7 Brush lightly with olive oil and bake for 25 minutes, or until the loaf sounds hollow when tapped on the base. Leave to cool on a wire rack.

Cheese and Onion Herb Stick

An extremely tasty bread which is very good with soup or salads. Use a strong cheese to give the bread plenty of flavour.

**Makes 2 sticks, each
serving 4–6**
15ml/1 tbsp sunflower oil
1 red onion, chopped
450g/1lb/4 cups strong white
  bread flour
5ml/1 tsp salt
5ml/1 tsp mustard powder
10ml/2 tsp easy-blend (rapid-rise)
  dried yeast
45ml/3 tbsp chopped fresh herbs,
  such as thyme, parsley,
  marjoram or sage
75g/3oz/3/4 cup grated reduced-
  fat Cheddar cheese
300ml/1/2 pint/1 1/4 cups
  hand-hot water

1 Lightly oil two baking sheets. Heat the oil in a frying pan and fry the onion until well browned.

2 Sift the flour, salt and mustard powder into a mixing bowl. Stir in the yeast and herbs.

3 Set aside 30ml/2 tbsp of the cheese. Add the remainder to the flour mixture and make a well in the centre. Add the water and the fried onions and their oil. Stir the ingredients working from the inside outwards, gradually incorporating the flour, and mix to a soft dough, adding a little extra water if necessary.

4 Turn the dough on to a floured surface and knead for 5 minutes until smooth and elastic. Divide the mixture in half and roll each piece into a stick 30cm/12in in length.

5 Place each bread stick on a baking sheet, make diagonal cuts along the top and sprinkle with the reserved cheese. Cover and leave until doubled in size, about 1 1/2 hours. Meanwhile, preheat the oven to 220°C/425°F/Gas 7.

6 Bake the loaves for 25 minutes, or until the bread sounds hollow when tapped underneath. Leave on a wire rack to cool completely.

Saffron Focaccia Energy 1018kcal/4292kJ; Protein 22.1g; Carbohydrate 179.6g, of which sugars 6.7g; Fat 28.3g, of which saturates 4.1g; Cholesterol 0mg; Calcium 349mg; Fibre 8.7g; Sodium 1666mg.
Herb Stick Energy 154kcal/653kJ; Protein 5.6g; Carbohydrate 29.5g, of which sugars 0.8g; Fat 2.4g, of which saturates 0.8g; Cholesterol 3mg; Calcium 106mg; Fibre 1.2g; Sodium 43mg.

Potato Bread

Vegetables incorporated into loaves make a moist crumb and help to keep the bread longer. You could try this recipe with cooked and mashed carrot instead.

**Makes two 23 x 13cm/
9 x 5in loaves**

20ml/4 tsp active dried yeast

*250ml/8fl oz/1 cup
  lukewarm milk*
*225g/8oz potatoes, boiled
  (reserve 250ml/8fl oz/1 cup
  of the cooking liquid)*
30ml/2 tbsp oil
20ml/4 tsp salt
*850–900g/1lb 4oz–2lb/
  7½–8 cups strong white
  bread flour*

1 Combine the yeast and milk in a large bowl and leave to dissolve and for the yeast to become frothy, about 15 minutes. Meanwhile, mash the potatoes.

2 Add the potatoes, the oil and the salt to the yeast mixture and mix to combine thoroughly.

3 Stir in the reserved cooking water, then stir in the flour, in six separate batches, to form a stiff dough.

4 Knead on a lightly floured surface until smooth. This will take about 10 minutes. Return to the bowl, cover with clear film (plastic wrap), and leave in a warm place until doubled in size, about 1–1½ hours.

5 Knock back (punch down), then leave to rise again for 40 minutes, or until almost doubled in size.

6 Grease two 23 x 13cm/9 x 5in loaf tins (pans). Roll the dough into 20 small balls. Place two rows of balls in each tin. Leave until the dough has risen above the rims of the tins, about 1½ hours.

7 Meanwhile, preheat the oven to 200°C/400°F/Gas 6. Bake the dough for 10 minutes, then lower the heat to 190°C/375°F/Gas 5. Bake until the bases of the loaves sound hollow when tapped, about 40 minutes. Cool on a wire rack.

Soda Bread

Finding the bread bin empty need never be a problem when your repertoire includes a recipe for soda bread. It takes only a few minutes to make and needs no rising or proving.

Serves 8

*450g/1lb/4 cups plain
  (all-purpose) flour*
5ml/1 tsp salt
*5ml/1 tsp bicarbonate of soda
  (baking soda)*
5ml/1 tsp cream of tartar
*350ml/12fl oz/1½ cups
  buttermilk*

1 Preheat the oven to 220°C/425°F/Gas 7 and lightly flour a baking sheet.

2 Sift the flour, salt, bicarbonate of soda and cream of tartar into a mixing bowl and make a well in the centre.

3 Add the buttermilk to the dry ingredients and mix quickly to form a soft dough. Turn the dough on to a floured surface and knead lightly.

4 Shape into a round about 18cm/7in in diameter, and place on the baking sheet.

5 Cut a deep cross on top of the loaf and sprinkle it with a little flour.

6 Bake the soda bread for 25–30 minutes, then transfer to a wire rack to cool.

> **Cook's Tips**
> • *Soda bread needs a light hand. The ingredients should be bound together quickly in the bowl and kneaded very briefly. The aim is just to get rid of the largest cracks, as the dough becomes tough if handled for too long.*
> • *If possible, eat soda bread warm from the oven as it does not keep well.*

Potato Bread Energy 1693kcal/7186kJ; Protein 46.4g; Carbohydrate 356.3g, of which sugars 13.9g; Fat 19g, of which saturates 3.6g; Cholesterol 7mg; Calcium 754mg; Fibre 14.5g; Sodium 4011mg.
Soda Bread Energy 206kcal/875kJ; Protein 6.8g; Carbohydrate 45.6g, of which sugars 2.8g; Fat 0.9g, of which saturates 0.2g; Cholesterol 2mg; Calcium 132mg; Fibre 1.7g; Sodium 267mg.

Sage Soda Bread

This wonderful loaf, quite unlike bread made with yeast, has a velvety texture and a powerful sage aroma.

Makes one loaf
225g/8oz/2cups plain (all-purpose) wholemeal (whole-wheat) flour
115g/4oz/1 cup plain (all-purpose) flour
2.5ml/½ tsp salt
5ml/1 tsp bicarbonate of soda (baking soda)
30ml/2 tbsp shredded fresh sage
300–450ml/½–¾ pint/ 1¼–scant 2 cups buttermilk

1 Preheat the oven to 220°C/425°F/Gas 7. Lightly grease a baking sheet and set aside.

2 Sift the wholemeal and white flours with the salt and bicarbonate of soda into a large bowl.

3 Stir in the fresh sage and add enough buttermilk to make a soft dough. Do not overmix or the bread will be heavy.

4 Shape the dough into a round loaf and place on the lightly greased baking sheet.

5 Cut a cross in the top, cutting deep into the dough.

6 Bake in the oven for about 40 minutes, or until the loaf is well risen and sounds hollow when tapped on the base. Leave to cool on a wire rack.

> **Variations**
> • Try this loaf made with all white flour rather than wholemeal (whole-wheat) and white for a finer and lighter texture.
> • Fresh rosemary would also work well in place of the sage for this loaf.
> • You could form the dough into two smaller loaves and bake them for 25–30 minutes.
> • Fruit soda bread tastes great, too. In place of the sage add 150g/5oz/1 cup raisins.

Irish Soda Bread

Easy to make, this distinctive bread goes well with soup, cheese and traditional, rustic-style dishes.

Makes one loaf
275g/10oz/2½ cups plain (all-purpose) flour
150g/5oz/1¼ cups plain (all-purpose) wholemeal (whole-wheat) flour
5ml/1 tsp bicarbonate of soda (baking soda)
5ml/1 tsp salt
25g/1oz/2 tbsp butter or margarine, at room temperature
300ml/½ pint/1¼ cups buttermilk
15ml/1 tbsp plain (all-purpose) flour, for dusting

1 Preheat the oven to 200°C/400°F/Gas 6. Grease a baking sheet. Sift together the flours, bicarbonate of soda and salt.

2 Make a central well and add the butter or margarine and buttermilk. Working from the centre, stir to combine the ingredients until a soft dough is formed.

3 With floured hands, gather the dough into a ball. Knead for up to 3 minutes. Shape the dough into a large round.

4 Place on the baking sheet. Cut a cross in the top with a sharp knife and dust with the flour. Bake until brown, about 40–50 minutes. Transfer to a wire rack to cool.

> **Cook's Tips**
> • It is the acid in buttermilk that acts with the bicarbonate of soda to make traditional soda bread rise. Because the bread does not include yeast it is not given any rising time. In fact, it is important to put the bread into the oven as soon as the liquid is added, as the gases start to form immediately and the loaf will be heavy if you don't put it straight in the oven.
> • Soured cream or milk with 15ml/1 tbsp lemon juice can be used instead of buttermilk, but do not substitute plain milk for the buttermilk as this will not produce a successful loaf.

Irish Soda Energy 1778kcal/7532kJ; Protein 56.7g; Carbohydrate 335.4g, of which sugars 21.8g; Fat 32.7g, of which saturates 17.3g; Cholesterol 71mg; Calcium 828mg; Fibre 22.5g; Sodium 2259mg.
Sage Soda Energy 1186kcal/5041kJ; Protein 49.6g; Carbohydrate 246.3g, of which sugars 19.6g; Fat 7.3g, of which saturates 1.3g; Cholesterol 11mg; Calcium 613mg; Fibre 23.8g; Sodium 1125mg.

Sun-dried Tomato Plait

This makes a marvellous centrepiece for a summer buffet. If you only have dried tomatoes, soak them in a little boiling water for 15 minutes and add 15ml/ 1 tbsp oil to the mixture.

Serves 8–10
225g/8oz/2 cups strong
    wholemeal (whole-wheat) flour
225g/8oz/2 cups strong white
    bread flour
5ml/1 tsp salt
1.5ml/1/4 tsp ground black pepper
10ml/2 tsp easy-blend (rapid-rise)
    dried yeast
a pinch of sugar
300ml/1/2 pint/1 1/4 cups
    hand-hot water
115g/4oz/2 cups drained sun-dried
    tomatoes in oil, chopped, plus
    15ml/1 tbsp oil from the jar
25g/1oz/1/3 cup freshly grated
    Parmesan cheese
30ml/2 tbsp red pesto
2.5ml/1/2 tsp coarse sea salt

1 Oil a baking sheet. Put the wholemeal flour in a large bowl. Sift in the white flour, salt and pepper. Add the yeast and sugar.

2 Make a well in the centre and add the water, the sun-dried tomatoes, oil, Parmesan cheese and pesto. Gradually incorporate the flour and mix to a soft dough, adding a little extra water if necessary.

3 Turn the dough on to a floured surface and knead for 5 minutes until smooth and elastic. Shape into three 33cm/13in long sausages.

4 Dampen the ends of the three sausages. Press them together at one end, braid them loosely, then press them together at the other end. Transfer to the baking sheet, and cover and leave in a warm place until doubled in size, about 1 1/2 hours. Meanwhile, preheat the oven to 220°C/425°F/Gas 7.

5 Sprinkle the braid with coarse sea salt. Bake for 10 minutes, then lower the oven temperature to 200°C/400°F/Gas 6 and bake for a further 15–20 minutes, or until the loaf sounds hollow when tapped underneath. Leave on a wire rack to cool completely.

Courgette Crown Bread

Adding grated courgettes and cheese to a loaf mixture will keep it tasting fresher for longer.

Serves 8
450g/1lb/2 3/4 cups coarsely
    grated courgettes (zucchini)
salt
500g/1 1/4lb/5 cups strong white
    bread flour
2 sachets easy-blend (rapid-rise)
    dried yeast
60ml/4 tbsp freshly grated
    Parmesan cheese
ground black pepper
30ml/2 tbsp olive oil
lukewarm water, to mix
milk, to glaze
sesame seeds, to garnish

1 Spoon the courgettes into a colander, sprinkling them lightly with salt. Leave to drain for 30 minutes, then pat dry with kitchen paper.

2 Mix the flour, yeast and Parmesan cheese together and season with black pepper.

3 Stir in the oil and courgettes, and add enough lukewarm water to make a firm dough.

4 Knead the dough on a lightly floured surface until smooth. This will take about 10 minutes. Return to the mixing bowl, cover it with oiled clear film (plastic wrap) and leave it to rise in a warm place, until doubled in size, about 1 1/2 hours.

5 Meanwhile, grease and line a 23cm/9in round cake tin (pan). Preheat the oven to 200°C/400°F/Gas 6.

6 Knock back (punch down) the dough, and knead it lightly. Break into eight balls, roll each one and arrange them, touching, in the tin. Brush the tops with the milk glaze and sprinkle over the sesame seeds.

7 Allow to rise again for 1 hour, then bake for 25 minutes, or until golden brown. Cool slightly in the tin, then turn out on to a wire rack to cool completely.

Tomato Plait Energy 190kcal/804kJ; Protein 7.7g; Carbohydrate 33.5g, of which sugars 2.4g; Fat 3.7g, of which saturates 1.4g; Cholesterol 6mg; Calcium 110mg; Fibre 3g; Sodium 89mg.
Crown Bread Energy 271kcal/1144kJ; Protein 8.9g; Carbohydrate 49.6g, of which sugars 1.9g; Fat 5.4g, of which saturates 1.6g; Cholesterol 5mg; Calcium 162mg; Fibre 2.5g; Sodium 57mg.

Walnut Bread

This rich bread could be served at a dinner party with soup or the cheese course, or with a rustic ploughman's lunch.

Makes one loaf

420g/15oz/3²/₃ cups strong wholemeal (whole-wheat) bread flour

150g/5oz/1¼ cups strong white bread flour
12.5ml/2½ tsp salt
550ml/18fl oz/2¼ cups lukewarm water
15ml/1 tbsp clear honey
15ml/1 tbsp active dried yeast
150g/5oz/1 cup walnut pieces, plus more to decorate
1 beaten egg, to glaze

1 Combine the wholemeal and white flours and salt in a large bowl. Make a well in the centre and add 250ml/8fl oz/1 cup of the water, the honey and the yeast. Set aside until the yeast dissolves and becomes frothy.

2 Add the remaining water. With a wooden spoon, stir from the centre, incorporating flour with each turn, to obtain a smooth dough. Add more flour if the dough is too sticky and use your hands if the dough becomes too stiff to stir.

3 Transfer to a floured board and knead, adding flour if necessary, until the dough is smooth and elastic. This will take about 10 minutes. Place in a greased bowl and roll the dough around in the bowl to coat thoroughly on all sides. Cover with clear film (plastic wrap) and leave in a warm place until doubled in volume, about 1½ hours. Knock back (punch down) the dough and knead in the walnuts evenly.

4 Grease a baking sheet. Shape the dough into a round loaf and place on the baking sheet. Press in walnut pieces to decorate the top. Cover loosely with a damp cloth or clear film and leave to rise in a warm place until doubled in size, 25–30 minutes.

5 Preheat the oven to 220°C/425°F/Gas 7. With a sharp knife, score the top of the loaf. Brush with the egg glaze. Bake for 15 minutes. Lower the heat to 190°C/375°F/Gas 5 and bake until the base sounds hollow when tapped, about 40 minutes.

Pecan Nut Rye Bread

A tasty homespun loaf that recalls the old folk-cooking of the United States.

Makes two 21 x 11cm/ 8½ x 4½in loaves

25ml/1½ tbsp active dried yeast
700ml/22fl oz/2¾ cups lukewarm water

675g/1½lb/6 cups strong white bread flour
500g/1¼lb/5 cups rye flour
30ml/2 tbsp salt
15ml/1 tbsp clear honey
10ml/2 tsp caraway seeds, (optional)
115g/4oz/½ cup butter, at room temperature
225g/8oz pecan nuts, chopped

1 Combine the yeast and 120ml/4fl oz/½ cup of the water. Stir and leave for 15 minutes for the yeast to dissolve entirely and become frothy.

2 In the bowl of an electric mixer, combine the white and rye flours, salt, honey, caraway seeds and butter. With the dough hook, mix on low speed until well blended. Alternatively, use your hands to incorporate the liquid into the flour.

3 Add the yeast mixture and the remaining water and mix on medium speed, or use your hands, until the dough forms a ball. Transfer to a floured surface and knead in the chopped pecan nuts.

4 Return the dough to the bowl, cover with clear film (plastic wrap) and leave in a warm place until doubled, about 2 hours.

5 Grease two 21 x 11cm/8½ x 4½in loaf tins (pans). Knock back (punch down) the risen dough.

6 Divide the dough in half and form into two loaves. Place in the tins, seam sides down. Dust the tops with flour. Cover with oiled clear film and leave to rise in a warm place until doubled in volume, about 1 hour.

7 Preheat the oven to 190°C/375°F/Gas 5. Bake until the bases sound hollow when tapped, 45–50 minutes. Transfer to wire racks to cool completely.

Walnut Bread Energy 2786kcal/11722kJ; Protein 87.1g; Carbohydrate 393.2g, of which sugars 26g; Fat 107g, of which saturates 9.4g; Cholesterol 0mg; Calcium 489mg; Fibre 47g; Sodium 4941mg.
Rye Bread Energy 3213kcal/13513kJ; Protein 63g; Carbohydrate 464.6g, of which sugars 16g; Fat 135.5g, of which saturates 37.8g; Cholesterol 123mg; Calcium 633mg; Fibre 45g; Sodium 4293mg.

Corn Bread

Serve this bread as an accompaniment to a meal, with soup, or take it on a picnic.

Makes one 23 x 13cm/ 9 x 5in loaf

115g/4oz/1 cup plain (all-purpose) flour
65g/2½oz/generous ¼ cup caster (superfine) sugar
5ml/1 tsp salt
15ml/1 tbsp baking powder
175g/6oz/1½ cups cornmeal or polenta
350ml/12fl oz/1½ cups milk
2 eggs
75g/3oz/6 tbsp butter, melted
115g/4oz/½ cup margarine, melted

1 Preheat the oven to 200°C/400°F/Gas 6. Then line a 23 × 13cm/9 × 5in loaf tin (pan) with baking parchment and grease the paper.

2 Sift the flour, sugar, salt and baking powder into a mixing bowl. Add the cornmeal or polenta and stir to blend. Make a well in the centre. Whisk together the milk, eggs, melted butter and margarine. Pour the mixture into the well. Stir until just blended; do not overmix.

3 Pour into the tin and bake until a skewer inserted in the centre comes out clean, about 45 minutes. Serve hot or at room temperature.

Cook's Tip
Often a loaf tin (pan) needs only to be greased and have a long strip of baking parchment placed along the base and up the short sides of the tin. At other times, however, it is best to line the whole tin. To do this cut another strip of baking parchment the length of the base of the tin and long enough to come up the long sides of the tin. Grease the paper you have already laid in the base of the tin and then lay the other sheet on top, smoothing both pieces up the sides of the tin. Finally, grease the paper.

Spicy Corn Bread

An interesting variation on basic corn bread; adjust the number of chillies used according to taste.

Makes 9 squares

3 or 4 whole canned chillies, drained
2 eggs
475ml/16fl oz/2 cups buttermilk
50g/2oz/¼ cup butter, melted
50g/2oz/½ cup plain (all-purpose) flour
5ml/1 tsp bicarbonate of soda (baking soda)
10ml/2 tsp salt
175g/6oz/scant 1½ cups cornmeal or polenta
350g/12oz/2½ cups canned corn or frozen corn, thawed

1 Preheat the oven to 200°C/400°F/Gas 6. Line the base and sides of a 23cm/9in square cake tin (pan) with baking parchment and lightly grease the paper.

2 With a sharp knife, finely chop the canned chillies and set aside until needed.

3 In a large bowl, whisk the eggs until frothy, then whisk in the buttermilk. Add the melted butter.

4 Sift the flour, bicarbonate of soda and salt together into another large bowl. Fold the dry ingredients into the buttermilk mixture in three batches, then fold in the cornmeal or polenta in three batches. Finally, fold in the chillies and corn and gently mix to combine thoroughly.

5 Pour the mixture into the tin and bake until a skewer inserted in the centre comes out clean; about 25–30 minutes. Leave in the tin for 2–3 minutes before unmoulding. Cut into squares and serve warm.

Cook's Tip
Bicarbonate of soda (baking soda) is used with buttermilk in this and many other recipes because the two together produce carbon dioxide to make the dough rise.

Corn Bread Energy 3008kcal/12539kJ; Protein 52.7g; Carbohydrate 303.3g, of which sugars 87.7g; Fat 179.8g, of which saturates 46.1g; Cholesterol 561mg; Calcium 696mg; Fibre 7.4g; Sodium 1672mg.
Spicy Corn Bread Energy 213kcal/892kJ; Protein 6.7g; Carbohydrate 31.2g, of which sugars 6.2g; Fat 7.1g, of which saturates 3.4g; Cholesterol 56mg; Calcium 82mg; Fibre 1.1g; Sodium 614mg.

American-style Corn Sticks

These traditional corn sticks are quick and simple to make, and can be enjoyed simply spread with butter or with jam.

Makes 6
1 egg
120ml/4fl oz/½ cup milk

15ml/1 tbsp vegetable oil
115g/4oz/scant 1 cup cornmeal
  or polenta
50g/2oz/½ cup plain
  (all-purpose) flour
10ml/2 tsp baking powder
45ml/3 tbsp caster
  (superfine) sugar

1 Preheat the oven to 190°C/375°F/Gas 5. Grease a cast-iron corn-stick mould and heat in the oven.

2 Beat the egg in a small bowl. Stir in the milk and vegetable oil, and set aside.

3 In a mixing bowl, stir together the cornmeal or polenta, flour, baking powder and sugar. Pour in the egg mixture and stir with a wooden spoon to combine.

4 Spoon the mixture into the prepared mould. Bake until a skewer inserted in the centre of a corn stick comes out clean, about 25 minutes.

5 Cool in the mould on a wire rack for 10 minutes before unmoulding.

Cook's Tips
• The traditional way to make corn sticks is in a cast-iron corn-stick mould, which is heated in the oven before the mixture is added. A new mould needs to be seasoned before use. Grease it well with white vegetable fat (shortening) and then heat it in a hot oven for about 20 minutes. After use wash in warm soapy water and then grease before storing.
• If you do not have a corn-stick mould use éclair tins (pans) instead and reduce the cooking time by 10 minutes.

Savoury Corn Bread

This corn bread has the delicious addition of cheese.

Makes 9
2 eggs, lightly beaten
250ml/8fl oz/1 cup buttermilk
115g/4oz/1 cup plain
  (all-purpose) flour
115g/4oz/scant 1 cup cornmeal

10ml/2 tsp baking powder
2.5ml/½ tsp salt
15ml/1 tbsp caster
  (superfine) sugar
115g/4oz/1 cup grated
  Cheddar cheese
225g/8oz/1¼ cups corn, fresh
  or frozen and thawed

1 Preheat the oven to 200°C/400°F/Gas 6. Grease a 23cm/9in square baking tin (pan).

2 Combine the eggs and buttermilk in a small bowl and whisk until well mixed. Set aside.

3 In another bowl, stir together the flour, cornmeal, baking powder, salt and sugar.

4 Add the egg mixture to the dry ingredients and stir with a wooden spoon to combine thoroughly. Stir in the cheese and corn and combine.

5 Pour the mixture into the baking tin. Bake until a skewer inserted in the centre comes out clean, about 25 minutes.

6 Unmould the bread on to a wire rack and leave to cool. Cut into squares before serving.

Cook's Tip
Buttermilk is made from the skimmed milk which is left over after the fat from full cream (whole) milk has been skimmed off to be used for making butter. This skimmed milk is then soured by bacteria to produce buttermilk. Although the results are not quite the same, yogurt is sometimes mixed with sweet (fresh) milk and works in a similar way to buttermilk.

Corn Sticks Energy 167kcal/700kJ; Protein 4.4g; Carbohydrate 29.3g, of which sugars 8.9g; Fat 3.8g, of which saturates 0.7g; Cholesterol 33mg; Calcium 45mg; Fibre 0.7g; Sodium 21mg.
Corn Bread Energy 206kcal/866kJ; Protein 8.7g; Carbohydrate 28.9g, of which sugars 5.6g; Fat 6.4g, of which saturates 3.2g; Cholesterol 56mg; Calcium 155mg; Fibre 1g; Sodium 188mg.

Danish Wreath

This is a delicious sweet loaf for tea.

Serves 10–12
5ml/1 tsp active dried yeast
175ml/6fl oz/3/4 cup milk
50g/2oz/1/2 cup caster (superfine) sugar
450g/1lb/4 cups strong white bread flour
2.5ml/1/2 tsp salt
2.5ml/1/2 tsp vanilla extract
1 egg, beaten

225g/8oz/1 cup unsalted (sweet) butter
1 egg yolk beaten with 10ml/ 2 tsp water
115g/4oz/1 cup icing (confectioners') sugar

For the filling
200g/7oz/scant 1 cup soft dark brown sugar
5ml/1 tsp ground cinnamon
50g/2oz/1/3 cup walnuts or pecans, plus extra to decorate

1 Mix the yeast, milk and 2.5ml/1/2 tsp of the sugar in a small bowl. Leave for 15 minutes to dissolve. Mix the flour, sugar and salt. Make a well and add the yeast, vanilla and egg to make a rough dough. Knead until smooth, wrap in clear film (plastic wrap) and chill. Roll the butter between sheets of baking parchment to form two 15 × 10cm/6 × 4in rectangles. Roll the dough to a 30 × 20cm/12 × 8in rectangle. Place one butter rectangle in the centre. Fold the bottom third of dough over and seal the edge. Place the other butter rectangle on top and cover with the top third of the dough.

2 Roll the dough into a 30 × 20cm/12 × 8in rectangle. Fold into thirds. Wrap and chill for 30 minutes. Repeat twice more. After the third fold, chill for 1–2 hours. Grease a baking sheet. Roll out the dough to a 62 × 15cm/25 × 6in strip. Mix the filling ingredients and spread over, leaving a 1cm/1/2in edge. Roll the dough into a cylinder, place on the baking sheet in a circle and seal the edges. Cover and leave to rise for 45 minutes.

3 Preheat the oven to 200°C/400°F/Gas 6. Slash the top every 5cm/2in, cutting 1cm/1/2in deep. Brush with the egg and milk. Bake for 35–40 minutes, or until golden. Cool. To serve, mix the icing sugar with a little water, then drizzle over the wreath. Sprinkle with some nuts.

Kugelhopf

A traditional round moulded bread from Germany, flavoured with Kirsch or brandy.

Makes one ring loaf
100g/3¾oz/¾ cup raisins
15ml/1 tbsp Kirsch or brandy
15ml/1 tbsp easy-blend (rapid-rise) dried yeast
120ml/4fl oz/1/2 cup lukewarm water
115g/4oz/1/2 cup unsalted (sweet) butter, at room temperature
90g/3½oz/1/2 cup caster (superfine) sugar

3 eggs, at room temperature
grated rind of 1 lemon
5ml/1 tsp salt
2.5ml/1/2 tsp vanilla extract
425g/15oz/32/3 cups strong white bread flour
120ml/4fl oz/1/2 cup milk
25g/1oz/1/4 cup flaked (sliced) almonds
80g/3¼oz/generous 1/2 cup whole blanched almonds, chopped
icing (confectioners') sugar, for dusting

1 In a bowl, combine the raisins and Kirsch or brandy. Combine the yeast and water, stir and leave for 15 minutes until the yeast becomes frothy.

2 Cream the butter and sugar until thick and fluffy. Beat in the eggs, one at a time. Add the lemon rind, salt and vanilla extract. Stir in the yeast mixture.

3 Add the flour, alternating with the milk, until well blended. Cover and leave to rise in a warm place until doubled in volume, about 2 hours.

4 Grease a 2.75 litre/4½ pint/11¼ cup kugelhopf mould, then sprinkle the flaked almonds evenly over the base. Work the raisins and chopped almonds into the dough, then spoon into the mould.

5 Cover with clear film (plastic wrap), and leave to rise in a warm place until the dough almost reaches the top of the tin, about 1 hour.

6 Preheat the oven to 180°C/350°F/Gas 4. Bake until golden brown, about 45 minutes. If the top browns too quickly, cover with foil. Cool in the tin for 15 minutes, then turn out on to a wire rack. Dust the top lightly with icing sugar.

Danish Wreath Energy 361kcal/1520kJ; Protein 5.4g; Carbohydrate 61.8g, of which sugars 33.2g; Fat 11.9g, of which saturates 5.6g; Cholesterol 37mg; Calcium 94mg; Fibre 1.3g; Sodium 73mg.
Kugelhopf Energy 3828kcal/16069kJ; Protein 84.1g; Carbohydrate 501.5g, of which sugars 174.8g; Fat 175.7g, of which saturates 70.1g; Cholesterol 816mg; Calcium 1047mg; Fibre 22.9g; Sodium 1000mg.

Poppy Seed Rolls

Pile these soft rolls in a basket and serve them for breakfast or with dinner.

Makes 12
oil, for greasing
450g/1lb/4 cups strong white
    bread flour
5ml/1 tsp salt

5ml/1 tsp easy-blend (rapid-rise)
    dried yeast
300ml/½ pint/1¼ cups hand-hot
    skimmed milk
1 egg, beaten

For the topping
1 egg, beaten
poppy seeds

1 Lightly grease two baking sheets with oil. Sift the flour and salt into a mixing bowl.

2 Add the yeast. Make a well in the centre and pour in the milk and the egg. Stir from the centre outwards, gradually incorporating the flour and mixing to a soft dough.

3 Turn the dough on to a floured surface and knead for 5 minutes, or until smooth and elastic. Cut into 12 pieces and shape into rolls (make a variety of shapes or just simple round rolls if you prefer).

4 Place the rolls on the prepared baking sheets, cover loosely with clear film (plastic wrap), ballooning it to trap the air inside, and leave in a warm place until the rolls have doubled in size, about 1½ hours. Meanwhile, preheat the oven to 220°C/425°F/Gas 7.

5 Glaze the rolls with beaten egg, sprinkle with poppy seeds and bake for 12–15 minutes, or until golden brown. Transfer to a wire rack to cool completely.

> **Variations**
> Vary the toppings. Linseed, sesame and caraway seeds all look good; try adding caraway seeds to the dough, too, for extra crunch and flavour.

French Bread

For truly authentic bread you should use flour grown and milled in France.

Makes 2 loaves
15ml/1 tbsp active dried yeast
475ml/16fl oz/2 cups
    lukewarm water

15ml/1 tbsp salt
850–900g/1lb 14oz–2lb/
    7½–8 cups strong white
    bread flour
semolina or flour,
    for sprinkling

1 In a large bowl, combine the yeast and water, stir, and leave for 15 minutes for the yeast to dissolve and become frothy. Stir in the salt.

2 Add the flour, 150g/5oz/1¼ cups at a time, to obtain a smooth dough. Knead for 5 minutes.

3 Shape into a ball, place in a greased bowl and cover with clear film (plastic wrap). Leave to rise in a warm place until doubled in size, about 2–4 hours.

4 Knock back (punch down) the dough. On a lightly floured surface, shape the dough into two long loaves. Place on a baking sheet sprinkled with semolina or flour and leave to rise for 5 minutes.

5 Score the tops of the loaves diagonally with a sharp knife. Brush with water and place in a cold oven. Place an ovenproof pan of boiling water on the base of the oven and set the oven to 200°C/400°F/Gas 6. Bake the loaves until crusty and golden, about 40 minutes. Cool on a wire rack.

> **Cook's Tip**
> A pan of boiling water placed in the oven will ensure that you will get the traditional crusty top for your French bread. Bake the loaves at the top of the oven and use proper French bread tins (pans) if you can, as these keep the loaves in shape and are perforated to aid cooking.

Poppy Seed Rolls Energy 142kcal/603kJ; Protein 4.9g; Carbohydrate 30.2g, of which sugars 1.7g; Fat 1g, of which saturates 0.2g; Cholesterol 17mg; Calcium 85mg; Fibre 1.2g; Sodium 18mg.
French Bread Energy 1559kcal/6626kJ; Protein 48.1g; Carbohydrate 341.4g, of which sugars 17.6g; Fat 9.6g, of which saturates 3.4g; Cholesterol 14mg; Calcium 881mg; Fibre 13.2g; Sodium 3063mg.

Wholemeal Rolls

To add interest, make these individual rolls into different shapes if you wish.

Makes 12
15ml/2 tbsp active dried yeast
50ml/2fl oz/¼ cup
   lukewarm water
5ml/1 tsp caster (superfine) sugar
175ml/6fl oz/¾ cup
   lukewarm buttermilk
1.5ml/¼ tsp bicarbonate of soda
   (baking soda)
5ml/1 tsp salt
40g/1½oz/3 tbsp butter,
   at room temperature
200g/7oz/scant 1¾ cups strong
   wholemeal (whole-wheat)
   bread flour
150g/5oz/1¼ cups plain
   (all-purpose) flour
1 beaten egg, to glaze

1 In a large bowl, combine the yeast, water and sugar. Stir, and leave for 15 minutes to dissolve and for the yeast to become frothy.

2 Add the buttermilk, bicarbonate of soda, salt and butter, and stir to blend. Stir in the strong wholemeal bread flour. Add just enough of the plain flour to obtain a rough dough.

3 Knead on a floured surface until smooth. This will take about 10 minutes. Divide into three equal parts. Roll each into a cylinder, then cut into four pieces.

4 Grease a baking sheet. Form the pieces into torpedo shapes, place on the baking sheet, cover with a clean dish towel and leave in a warm place until doubled in size, about 1 hour.

5 Preheat the oven to 200°C/400°F/Gas 6. Brush the rolls with egg. Bake until firm, about 15–20 minutes. Cool on a wire rack.

Cook's Tip
Kneading is the most important part of breadmaking, as it develops the dough and helps it to rise. You can be as rough as you like: make the dough into a ball and then press down and push it away from you with one hand, so that it stretches. Repeat until the dough is elastic.

Granary Baps

These baps make excellent picnic fare and are also good buns for hamburgers.

Makes 8
oil, for greasing
450g/1lb/4 cups malted
   brown flour
5ml/1 tsp salt
10ml/2 tsp easy-blend (rapid-rise)
   dried yeast
15ml/1 tbsp malt extract
300ml/½ pint/1¼ cups
   hand-hot water
15ml/1 tbsp rolled oats

1 Lightly oil a large baking sheet. Put the malted flour, salt and yeast in a large bowl and make a well in the centre. Dissolve the malt extract in the water and add it to the well.

2 Stir from the centre outwards, gradually incorporating the flour and mixing to a soft dough.

3 Turn the dough on to a floured surface and knead for 5 minutes, or until smooth and elastic. Divide the dough into eight pieces.

4 Shape into balls and flatten with the palm of your hand to make 10cm/4in rounds.

5 Place the rounds on the prepared baking sheet, cover loosely with oiled clear film (plastic wrap) (ballooning it to trap the air inside) and leave in a warm place until the baps have doubled in size. Preheat the oven to 220°C/425°F/Gas 7.

6 Brush the baps with water, sprinkle with the oats and bake for 20–25 minutes, or until they sound hollow when tapped underneath. Cool on a wire rack.

Variation
To make a large loaf, shape the dough into a round, flatten it slightly and bake for 30–40 minutes. Test by tapping the base of the loaf – if it sounds hollow, it is cooked.

Wholemeal Rolls Energy 127kcal/538kJ; Protein 3.8g; Carbohydrate 21.5g, of which sugars 1.7g; Fat 3.5g, of which saturates 2g; Cholesterol 8mg; Calcium 42mg; Fibre 1.9g; Sodium 27mg.
Granary Baps Energy 195kcal/834kJ; Protein 7.3g; Carbohydrate 41.4g, of which sugars 2.4g; Fat 1.3g, of which saturates 0.2g; Cholesterol 0mg; Calcium 75mg; Fibre 3.7g; Sodium 254mg.

Wholemeal Herb Triangles

These make a good lunchtime snack when stuffed with ham and salad and also taste good when served with soup.

Makes 8

225g/8oz/2 cups strong wholemeal (whole-wheat) bread flour
115g/4oz/1 cup strong white bread flour
5ml/1 tsp salt
2.5ml/½ tsp bicarbonate of soda (baking soda)
5ml/1 tsp cream of tartar
2.5ml/½ tsp chilli powder
50g/2oz/¼ cup soft margarine
250ml/8fl oz/1 cup skimmed milk
60ml/4 tbsp chopped mixed fresh herbs
15ml/1 tbsp sesame seeds

1 Preheat the oven to 220°C/425°F/Gas 7. Lightly flour a baking sheet.

2 Put the wholemeal flour in a large bowl. Sift in the strong white bread flour, the salt, bicarbonate of soda, cream of tartar and the chilli powder, then rub in the margarine.

3 Add the milk and herbs and mix quickly to a soft dough. Turn on to a lightly floured surface. Knead only very briefly or the dough will become tough.

4 Roll out to a 23cm/9in circle and place on the prepared baking sheet. Brush lightly with water and sprinkle with the sesame seeds.

5 Cut the dough round into 8 wedges, separate slightly and bake for 15–20 minutes. Transfer the triangles to a wire rack to cool. Serve warm or cold.

> **Variation**
> Sun-dried Tomato Triangles: replace the mixed herbs with 30ml/2 tbsp chopped, drained sun-dried tomatoes in oil, and add 15ml/1 tbsp mild paprika, 15ml/1 tbsp chopped fresh parsley and 15ml/1 tbsp chopped fresh marjoram.

Poppy Seed Knots

The poppy seeds look attractive and add a slightly nutty flavour to these rolls.

Makes 12

300ml/½ pint/1¼ cups lukewarm milk
50g/2oz/¼ cup butter, at room temperature
5ml/1 tsp caster (superfine) sugar
10ml/2 tsp active dried yeast
1 egg yolk
10ml/2 tsp salt
500–575g/1¼lb–1lb 6oz/ 5–5½ cups strong white bread flour
1 egg beaten with 10ml/2 tsp water, to glaze
poppy seeds, for sprinkling

1 In a large bowl, stir together the milk, butter, sugar and yeast. Leave for 15 minutes to dissolve and for the yeast to become frothy.

2 Stir in the egg yolk, salt and 275g/10oz/2½ cups of the flour. Add half the remaining flour and stir to obtain a soft dough.

3 Transfer the dough to a floured surface and knead, adding flour if necessary, until smooth and elastic. This will take about 10 minutes.

4 Place in a bowl, cover with clear film (plastic wrap) and leave in a warm place until the dough doubles in volume, about 1½–2 hours.

5 Grease a baking sheet. Knock back (punch down) the dough with your fist and cut into 12 pieces the size of golf balls.

6 Roll each piece into a rope, twist to form a knot and place 2.5cm/1in apart on the prepared baking sheet. Cover loosely and leave to rise in a warm place until doubled in volume, about 1–1½ hours.

7 Meanwhile, preheat the oven to 180°C/350°F/Gas 4. Brush the knots with the egg glaze and sprinkle over the poppy seeds. Bake until the tops are lightly browned, about 30 minutes. Cool slightly on a wire rack before serving.

Herb Triangles Energy 204kcal/858kJ; Protein 6.3g; Carbohydrate 30.6g, of which sugars 2.3g; Fat 7.1g, of which saturates 0.3g; Cholesterol 1mg; Calcium 82mg; Fibre 3.1g; Sodium 65mg.
Poppy Seed Knots Energy 191kcal/807kJ; Protein 5g; Carbohydrate 33.9g, of which sugars 2.2g; Fat 4.9g, of which saturates 2.7g; Cholesterol 27mg; Calcium 91mg; Fibre 1.3g; Sodium 366mg.

Breadsticks

If you prefer, use other seeds, such as poppy seeds, in these sticks.

Makes 18–20
15ml/1 tbsp active dried yeast
300ml/½ pint/1¼ cups
   lukewarm water
425g/15oz/3⅔ cups strong white
   bread flour
10ml/2 tsp salt
5ml/1 tsp caster (superfine) sugar
30ml/2 tbsp olive oil
1 egg, beaten, to glaze
150g/5oz/10 tbsp sesame
   seeds, toasted
coarse salt, for sprinkling

1 Combine the yeast and water in a small bowl, stir and leave for about 15 minutes for the yeast to dissolve and become frothy.

2 Place the flour, salt, sugar and olive oil in a food processor. With the motor running, slowly pour in the yeast mixture and process until the dough forms a ball. Alternatively, use your hand to incorporate the liquid into the flour.

3 Knead until smooth. This will take about 10 minutes. Place in a bowl, cover with clear film (plastic wrap) and leave to rise in a warm place for 45 minutes. Grease two baking sheets.

4 Roll the dough into 18–20 30cm/12in sticks. Place on the baking sheets, brush with the egg glaze then sprinkle with toasted sesame seeds and coarse salt. Leave to rise, uncovered, for 20 minutes.

5 Preheat the oven to 200°C/400°F/Gas 6. Bake until golden, about 15 minutes. Turn off the heat but leave in the oven for a further 5 minutes. Serve warm or cool.

> **Variation**
> For Rye and Caraway Breadsticks, substitute 200g/7oz/scant 2 cups rye flour for 200g/7oz/scant 2 cups of the strong white bread flour. Sprinkle with caraway seeds instead of sesame seeds.

Caraway Breadsticks

Ideal to nibble with drinks, these can be made in a wide variety of flavours, including cumin seed, poppy seed and celery seed, as well as the coriander and sesame variation given below.

Makes about 20
225g/8oz/2 cups plain
   (all-purpose) flour
2.5ml/½ tsp salt
2.5ml/½ tsp easy-blend
   (rapid-rise) dried yeast
10ml/2 tsp caraway seeds
150ml/¼ pint/⅔ cup
   hand-hot water
a pinch of sugar

1 Grease two baking sheets. Sift the flour, salt, yeast and sugar into a large bowl, stir in the caraway seeds and make a well in the centre.

2 Add the water and stir from the centre outwards, gradually mixing the flour to make a soft dough, and adding a little extra water if necessary.

3 Turn the dough on to a lightly floured surface and knead for 5 minutes until smooth and elastic.

4 Divide the mixture into 20 pieces and roll each one into a 30cm/12in stick.

5 Arrange the breadsticks on the baking sheets, leaving room to allow for rising. Leave for 30 minutes, or until well risen. Meanwhile, preheat the oven to 220°C/425°F/Gas 7.

6 Bake the breadsticks for 10–12 minutes, or until golden brown. Cool on the baking sheets.

> **Variation**
> To make Coriander and Sesame Sticks: replace the caraway seeds with 15ml/1 tbsp crushed coriander seeds. Dampen the breadsticks lightly and sprinkle with sesame seeds before baking.

Breadsticks Energy 128kcal/538kJ; Protein 3.4g; Carbohydrate 16.8g, of which sugars 0.6g; Fat 5.7g, of which saturates 0.8g; Cholesterol 0mg; Calcium 80mg; Fibre 1.3g; Sodium 199mg.
Caraway Breadsticks Energy 41kcal/176kJ; Protein 1.2g; Carbohydrate 8.7g, of which sugars 0.2g; Fat 0.4g, of which saturates 0.1g; Cholesterol 0mg; Calcium 19mg; Fibre 0.4g; Sodium 50mg.

Croissants

Enjoy breakfast Continental-style with these melt-in-the-mouth croissants.

Makes 18
15ml/1 tbsp active dried yeast
325ml/11fl oz/1⅓ cups
   lukewarm milk
10ml/2 tsp caster (superfine) sugar
12.5ml/1½ tsp salt
450g/1lb/4 cups strong white
   bread flour
225g/8oz/1 cup cold unsalted
   (sweet) butter
1 egg, beaten with 10ml/2 tsp
   water, to glaze

1 In a large bowl, stir together the yeast and milk. Leave for about 15 minutes for the yeast to become frothy. Stir in the sugar and salt, and about 150g/5oz/1¼ cups of the flour.

2 Slowly add the remaining flour. Mix well until the dough pulls away from the sides of the bowl. Cover and leave to rise in a warm place until doubled in size, about 1½ hours.

3 Turn out on to a lightly floured surface and knead until smooth. Wrap in baking parchment and chill for 15 minutes.

4 Roll out the butter between two sheets of baking parchment to make two 15 × 10cm/6 × 4in rectangles. Roll out the dough to a 30 × 20cm/12 × 8in rectangle.

5 Interleave the butter with the dough. With a short side facing you, roll it out again to 30 × 20cm/12 × 8in. Fold in thirds again, wrap and chill for 30 minutes. Repeat this procedure twice, then chill for 2 hours.

6 Roll out the dough to a rectangle about 3mm/⅛in thick. Trim the sides, and then cut into 18 equal-size triangles. Roll up from the base to the point. Place point-down on baking sheets and curve to form crescents. Cover and leave to rise in a warm place until more than doubled in size, about 1–1½ hours.

7 Preheat the oven to 240°C/475°F/Gas 9. Brush with egg glaze. Bake for 2 minutes. Lower the heat to 190°C/375°F/Gas 5 and bake until golden, about 10–12 minutes. Serve warm.

Tomato Breadsticks

Once you've tried this exceptionally simple recipe you'll never buy manufactured breadsticks again.

Makes 16
225g/8oz/2 cups strong white
   bread flour
2.5ml/½ tsp salt
7.5ml/½ tbsp easy-blend
   (rapid-rise) dried yeast
5ml/1 tsp honey
5ml/1 tsp olive oil
150ml/¼ pint/⅔ cup
   warm water
6 halves sun-dried tomatoes in
   olive oil, drained and chopped
15ml/1 tbsp milk
10ml/2 tsp poppy seeds

1 Place the flour, salt and yeast in a food processor. Add the honey and olive oil and, with the machine running, gradually pour in the water until the dough starts to cling together (you may not need all the water).

2 Process for a further 1 minute. Alternatively, use your hand to incorporate the liquid into the flour.

3 Turn out the dough on to a floured surface and knead for 3–4 minutes, until springy and smooth. Knead in the sun-dried tomatoes.

4 Form the dough into a ball and place in a lightly oiled bowl. Cover with clear film (plastic wrap). Place in a warm position and leave to rise for 5 minutes.

5 Preheat the oven to 150°C/300°F/Gas 2. Lightly grease a baking sheet. Divide the dough into 16 pieces and roll each piece into a 28 × 1cm/11 × ½in stick.

6 Place on the lightly greased baking sheet and leave to rise in a warm place for 15 minutes.

7 Brush the breadsticks with milk and sprinkle with poppy seeds. Bake for 30 minutes. Leave the breadsticks to cool on a wire rack.

Tomato Breadsticks Energy 53kcal/227kJ; Protein 1.5g; Carbohydrate 11.7g, of which sugars 1g; Fat 0.4g, of which saturates 0.1g; Cholesterol 0mg; Calcium 22mg; Fibre 0.5g; Sodium 68mg.
Croissants Energy 189kcal/789kJ; Protein 3g; Carbohydrate 20.9g, of which sugars 1.9g; Fat 10.9g, of which saturates 6.8g; Cholesterol 28mg; Calcium 59mg; Fibre 0.8g; Sodium 357mg.

Index

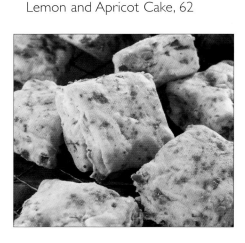